OTHER BOOKS FROM THE BRAVE GIRLS

This Journal Belongs to

Clara

From

CSBC

Date

December 2021
Merry Christmas!

TOMMY NELSON'S BRAVE GIRLS

I Am
BRAVE

Tommy NELSON®

An Imprint of Thomas Nelson

I Am Brave

© 2019 by Thomas Nelson

Published in Nashville, Tennessee, by Tommy Nelson. Tommy Nelson is an imprint of Thomas Nelson. Thomas Nelson is a registered trademark of HarperCollins Christian Publishing, Inc.

Published in association with the literary agency of Folio Literary Management, LLC.

Cover design by Micah Kandros

Illustrations by Aleksey and Olga Ivanov

Unless otherwise noted, Scripture quotations are taken from the International Children's Bible®. Copyright © 1986, 1988, 1999, 2015 by Thomas Nelson. Used by permission. All rights reserved.

Scripture quotations marked NKJV are taken from the New King James Version®. © 1982 by Thomas Nelson. Used by permission. All rights reserved.

Scripture quotations marked NLT are taken from the Holy Bible, New Living Translation. © 1996, 2004, 2007, 2013, 2015 by Tyndale House Foundation. Used by permission of Tyndale House Publishers, Inc., Carol Stream, Illinois 60188. All rights reserved.
ISBN-13: 978-1-4002-1192-0

Library of Congress Cataloging-in-Publication Data is on File

Printed in China

19 20 21 22 23 DSC 5 4 3 2 1

Mfr: DSC / Shenzhen, China / August 2019 / PO #9541184

MEET THE BRAVE GIRLS

Ready for a game of football? Yeah, I know I'm a girl. And girls aren't supposed to play football, right? Well, you haven't seen me with my brothers. Every Saturday afternoon we're out in the yard playing flag football with our neighbors. And if it isn't football, it's soccer or softball. We even have a volleyball net! I guess that's one advantage to living on a farm outside of town—plenty of room to play hard.

I actually have a girly side to me that likes to dress up and be pretty and all that stuff. But give me a pair of broken-in jeans, a T-shirt, and a good group of friends, and I'm happier than a homecoming queen.

I guess you could say nothing in my life is all that fancy. Farm life just isn't that way. But I have a terrific family. I'm the oldest, and my two younger brothers are twins my parents adopted from Ukraine when they were two years old. I love those guys, even though they bother me sometimes. We all work together around the farm and around our church. We help out with the local charity too because we can't get over how good God has been to us. And sharing His hope with others? Well, it beats football any day.

I do admit that I have a challenge I don't like to talk about: reading. I do okay in school for the most part. But when I read, the letters get mixed up, and sometimes it looks like another language to me. They call it dyslexia. I call it embarrassing. But I do my best to remember that God can help me tackle this challenge. And He's where I'm learning to put my—you guessed it—hope!

Glory

If you could be anywhere in the world right now, where would you be? I'm kind of torn. Half of me would want to be on a high mountain somewhere, enjoying a beautiful sunset. Or maybe the beach, looking out across the sparkling waters. But the other half of me would be just as wonderstruck walking down the streets of New York City with my mom and sisters, shopping for all the latest fashions! I mean, you can never have enough boots, right? Or scarves and earrings and nail polish to match?

Yes, I know it might sound weird, but there is a common thread to everything I love: beauty! I love beauty wherever I see it: in this awesome world God created, in a gorgeous dress in a store window, and in the great hugs I get from my friends. I think God's beauty is everywhere—you just have to look for it.

Lately, I've had to look a little harder. Life at home wasn't so pretty, and just last summer my parents got divorced. For a while, I got really mad at God and forgot about the good in the world. But then my friends from the youth group started writing me encouraging notes and inviting me over. Their love and friendship was, well, beautiful—and it got me noticing all the other amazing ways God shows His love to me. I've started to see how God can take even the ugly, hard things in life and turn them into something good. I'm working on forgiving my parents and praying that God will use me to encourage other girls like me. You know, God can take even the messiest of situations and use them for His glory!

My friends say that whenever and wherever there's a challenge, I'm the one to take it! Maybe that's why I always pick up stray animals and bring them home. I love to care for my furry friends and figure out how to make them better. I'm always going to the library to find new books to help me in my animal rescue mission! In fact, I love to read books in general. Last summer I started volunteering at the library so that I could help other kids learn to love books too.

But my biggest challenge lately hasn't been at the library or with my five pets. It's been at school. Studying has always been easy for me, and I was thrilled when the principal said I could skip a grade. But I had a really hard time fitting in with the older kids. They didn't seem impressed with my intelligence, so at first I tried dressing and talking more like they did, even though I knew it didn't honor God. That didn't work either.

I just ended up feeling guilty and more out of place than ever. Turns out they weren't the kind of friends I needed anyway. It's a good thing God has given me an awesome youth group. My leader and friends there have helped me remember who God says I am.

So who am I, really? You could say I'm God's girl, even though I don't *always* act like it. But I am learning how to honor Him more. And one day I hope to take all the abilities God has given me and use them, maybe to become a veterinarian or zoologist or something. Whatever I do, though, one thing's for sure: I want it all to honor God.

GRacie

Let's just say it's all by God's grace that I'm here. And I'm not just saying that because of my name. If it had been left up to me, I'd still be in my old hometown of Perkasie, Pennsylvania. We're talking beautiful green hills and parks on every street corner. I was born there, and I knew everybody (and everybody knew me).

And then we moved. I thought life was over. I wanted my old friends and old world back, and I was pretty stubborn and loud about it.

In my hometown, my family and I didn't talk about God much. But once we moved here, we started going to this church, and there were some girls in the youth group who were . . . nice. More than nice, really. They were cool. They liked to do fun stuff and all, but they also weren't afraid to talk about things that matter— like what we're supposed to do with our lives. I used to ask myself that question sometimes, like when I was walking through the woods by my house or listening to my music. These girls were able to show me the answer in the Bible. I always knew there had to be a God who made all those beautiful things. Now I'm beginning to know who He is, thanks to God Himself, those girls, my church, and, yes, even my parents, who moved me here.

Wanna know something else kind of funny? The only time I ever sang back in Pennsylvania was in my shower at home. I loved it, but I was afraid to sing in public. Now I'm in the choir at church, and I'm singing about God to anybody who'll listen!

Have you ever known anybody who is homeschooled? If you haven't, now you do! My sister and I have been homeschooled all our lives. I miss my friends, but I still love learning at home because I have more time—to finish my work, to hang out, and to think. I've even used that time to start reading the Bible on my own because I really want to make God happy.

But to tell you the truth, I tend to try to please more than just God. I want everyone to like what I do, which has made me quite a perfectionist. Even though my name is Faith, I think a better name right now would be Worry because I'm always worried that I'm going to disappoint someone, including myself. The only time I get away from those thoughts is when I'm painting, my favorite hobby. Fortunately, I find lots of time for that, which is starting to pay off. I've been asked to help the younger kids with their art projects at camp this year, and I've even won some local art contests!

The girls in the youth group are helping me too, and I love spending time with them. They remind me that God already knows all about my mess-ups and sins but loves me anyway. I guess I'm learning that my faith is not a bunch of "dos and don'ts." It's about a relationship with God, who knows the *real* me, and He is working on me to make me more like Him. That's what real faith is all about—believing that God loves me, forgives me, and sees me as His very own work of art, no matter what!

If God had thought we worked better alone, He wouldn't have invited so many people into His family. We need each other! Just like a body works best when all its parts are connected, God's family is the strongest when all His kids work and worship together.

But a funny thing often happens with a big group of people who spend a lot of time together. The people start to look the same. They dress the same, talk the same, and only welcome other people who are, well, just like them. Think about your body: Can you imagine if your nose decided to be an eye instead? And then, out of peer pressure, your ear became an eye, then your hands, and . . . you get the picture. You'd have a body of eyes without any ability to move, feel, taste, touch, or smell. Plus, you'd creep out a lot of people.

Each one of us has a special way to honor God and help others see Him in ways the rest of us can't on our own. But together, we're even stronger—which is a great part of God's plan.

That's what our youth group is all about: learning how to work together to know God better and to tell other people about Him too. We meet every week to talk, to learn what God is saying to us in the Bible, and to pray about anything and everything—together, the way God's family was meant to be. Want to join us?

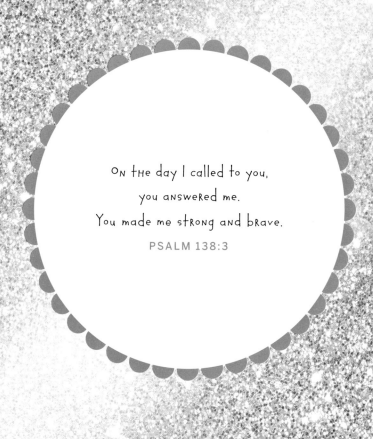

On the day I called to you,
you answered me.
You made me strong and brave.

PSALM 138:3

INTRODUCING . . . ME!

I pRaise you because you made me in
an amazing and wonderful way.

PSALM 139:14

Draw a picture of yourself—or attach a selfie—here.

RIPPLE EFFECT

"He who believes in me will do the
same things that I do."

JOHN 14:12

Have you ever thrown a rock into a still lake? If so, you've seen the "ripple effect." Rings of waves flow from the spot where your rock landed, making bigger and bigger circles the farther they travel. It's amazing how one little rock can have such a big impact!

In a way, the world is like that lake. It may seem too big, and you may feel too small for your life to make an impact. But God doesn't see you that way. He uses everything you do, no matter how small, to impact the world. The effects of your actions can reach places you never could've imagined.

How can you be like a rock that causes waves of good wherever you go? Maybe it's as simple as helping your mom carry in the groceries. Or asking that girl who just moved into your neighborhood to hang out. Or posting a Bible verse on your locker for everyone to see. It may take some courage but be brave. "Rock" this world—and see how God uses the ripple effect in your life.

A BRAVE GIRL'S PRAYER

Lord, give me the courage to impact this world for You.

ALL ABOUT Me!

Every Brave Girl is a one-of-a-kind, amazing masterpiece created by God Himself—including you. Tell all about yourself!

My name is _____

My friends call me _____

My family calls me _____

My hair is _____

My eyes are _____

My birthday is _____

I was born in _____

I am _____ years old.

I'm in the _____ grade.

My school is _____

My church is _____

My hobbies and sports are _____

_____

WHAT'S IT MEAN?

All you who put your hope in the
Lord be strong and brave.

PSALM 31:24

What does the word **brave** mean to you? _____

_____

What about **courage**? What does it mean to you? _____

_____

What do you think these words mean to God? (Use Bible verses to back
up your answer. Find verses by looking in your Bible's concordance, or
search an online Bible using the keywords **brave** and **courage**.)

_____

_____

IT'S UP TO YOU

I pRay tHat tHe God wHo gives Hope will fill you with mucH joy and peace wHile you tRust iN Him.

ROMANS 15:13

Every day you have choices to make. Which clothes should you wear? Which shoes work best with your outfit? Should you put your hair in a ponytail? Then there's breakfast to figure out—and you haven't even left the house yet!

But there's one choice you can make every morning, even before you even get out of bed: choose to be brave. Yep, brave. You see, lots of things happen in our days—good things, bad things, exciting things, boring things, and thousands of other things in between. And while you may not control everything that happens, you get to choose how you let those things affect you, and also what you're going to do about them. What if someone asks you to do something you know is wrong, but you don't want to hurt her feelings?

Some days will require a bit more courage and determination than others. But if you choose to be brave and focus on showing God and His love to others, then you'll be off to an amazing start! So when you wake up in the morning, yawn and stretch—and choose to be brave. After all, it's your choice.

A BRaVe GiRL'S PRayeR

LoRd, I want to be bRave foR You. OpeN my eyes to see all tHe ways I can sHaRe You and YouR love iN tHis woRld.

•5•

BEGIN THE DAY BRAVE!

Depend on the Lord. Trust Him, and
He will take care of you.

PSALM 37:5

Before you head out for the day, check through this list to make sure you're setting yourself up to begin the day brave!

❑ Pray and say good morning to God!

❑ Pick a verse for the day. Read it and talk to God about it.

❑ Brush your teeth and ask God to help you watch your words.

❑ Wash your face and ask God to wash away your sins.

❑ Get dressed for the day and ask God to clothe you with His protection.

❑ Grab some breakfast and ask God to fill you with His Spirit.

❑ Hug your family and thank God for all your blessings.

❑ Plan to do at least one brave thing today.

❑ Make a plan for when you're tempted to do or say something you shouldn't.

❑ Head out and ask God to guide your steps all throughout the day.

A Giggle a Day

I will be happy because of you. God Most
High, I will sing praises to your name.

PSALM 9:2

You've probably heard the saying "an apple a day keeps the doctor away." Well, a happy heart just might do the same. God says a happy heart is like medicine for our body and our soul. So what's the secret? How do we have a happy heart—especially on days that don't feel so happy?

It's simple: choose to see God and all that is good. Even on the worst days, you have so many things to be thankful for. There are all those things you can see, like home and family and friends. And then there are the things you can know, like the fact that God loves you, no matter what. You might need a bit of strength and courage to make yourself look around and find it, but God's goodness is always there.

One way God shows His love is by filling this world with wonderful things—even things that make you giggle and laugh. Have you ever watched a puppy play or *really* looked at a giraffe? God definitely has a sense of humor! So get yourself happy heart . . . ask God to help you find something to giggle about every day!

A Brave Girl's Prayer

Lord, thank You for giggles. Help me find
things to be happy about every day.

SO FUNNY!

There is a time . . . to laugh. . . .
and a time to dance.

ECCLESIASTES 3:4

The most I've ever laughed _____

_____

I always laugh when _____

_____

The funniest joke _____

_____

The worst joke _____

_____

My friends and I still laugh about _____

_____

_____

_____

Attach a picture of your *craziest* selfie here.

THINGS I LOVE

He fills my life with good things.

PSALM 103:5 NLT

My favorite color _____

My favorite smell _____

My favorite sound _____

My favorite class _____

My favorite teacher _____

My favorite book _____

My favorite word _____

My favorite movie _____

My favorite TV show _____

My favorite song _____

My favorite holiday _____

My favorite thing to do _____

My favorite place to hang out _____

My favorite picture of me _____

My favorite Bible verse _____

My favorite thing about God _____

My favorite place to talk to God _____

IT DEPENDS

By His power we live and move and exist.

ACTS 17:28

You've probably said it a million times to your parents: "I can do this myself!" We all want to show our family and friends that we're growing up and getting better at life. We feel proud when we're able to do things on our own. And that's natural.

But growing up as a Christian should be exactly the opposite. God wants us to learn more and more about how much we *do* need Him. We can't do anything that's truly important on our own. The Bible even says that apart from God, we can do nothing (John 15:5). We depend on God for everything—including His help to make us brave when we need to be—and that's a beautiful thing.

What do you depend on God for? Here is a list of some things. Can you think of more?

- the wisdom to know what's right
- the courage to choose what's right

- growing my faith
- fighting temptation
- knowing how to pray
- loving others well

A BRAVE GIRL'S PRAYER

Lord, I'm so excited about getting older and doing new things. Help me never forget I'll always need You.

COURAGEOUS CHARACTER

Create in me a pure heart, God.
Make my spirit right again.

PSALM 51:10

God wants you to show His goodness and love to the world around you. Are there ways you can show God's love to others? Are there things you need to work on, such as being selfless, thankful, and forgiving? Be brave enough to admit there are areas you need to work on. List those thoughts here, and then talk to God about them in prayer.

WE ARE FAMILY

We should love each other, because love
comes from God. The person who loves has
become God's child and knows God.

1 JOHN 4:7

When you think of the word **family**, what words come to mind?

_____

How would you describe your family? _____

_____

What's the very best thing about your family? _____

_____

Is there anything you'd like to change? _____

_____

How does your family help you be brave? _____

_____

FAMILY FACTS

If we love each other, God lives in us.

WHO ARE THE people iN youR family? _____

_____

_____

List THRee fabulous facts about youR family.

1. _____

2. _____

3. _____

List THRee weiRD aND fuNNy facts about youR family.

1. _____

2. _____

3. _____

Attach or draw a picture of your family here.

MORE THAN A BOOK

Use the shield of faith. With that you can
stop all the burning arrows of the Evil One.

EPHESIANS 6:16

Did you know you're in the middle of a war? It's a war with Satan, and he's attacking all the time. One of his favorite weapons is telling lies—after all, he's the father of lies. He shoots them like arrows, straight at your heart. But don't worry! Your faith is your shield. When you believe the promises of God's Word, you are protected from Satan's lies.

- Satan says you're not good enough, but God says you're amazing and wonderful (Psalm 139:14).

- Satan says you're a nobody, but God says you're His very own child when you follow Him (John 1:12).

- Satan says you're not pretty enough, but God says everything about you is beautiful (Song of Solomon 4:7).

- Satan says nobody cares about you, but God says He loves you so much He sent His Son to save you (John 3:16).

When Satan's ugly lies start to haunt you, pick up your shield and let God's Word protect you. Make time to read your Bible, study it, and memorize its words. The Bible isn't just another book—it's your shield.

A BRAVE GIRL'S PRAYER

Thank You, Lord, for shielding me.

DEFEATING THE LIES

It is our faith that wins the
victory against the world.

1 JOHN 5:4

Just like an arrow, some of Satan's lies can really hit their mark. List the lies the devil likes to tell you. But don't believe them! Defeat each lie by drawing a line right through it, and then writing out God's truth.

The devil's lie: _____

_____

God's truth: _____

_____

The devil's lie: _____

_____

God's truth: _____

_____

The devil's lie: _____

_____

God's truth: _____

_____

READ ALL ABOUT . . .
BRAVE GIRLS!

My favorite heroine from a book _____

_____

The thing I love most about her _____

_____

I admire her because _____

_____

The most amazing part of her story was when _____

_____

One way I am like her _____

_____

One way I wish I were more like her _____

_____

SUPER STAR POWER

G rab some popcorn and a friend—and watch a movie starring your favorite, saves-the-day heroine!

My favorite movie HeRoine is _____

_____

HeR gReatest cHallenge _____

_____

SHe saved tHe day by _____

_____

I most admiRe HeR foR HeR _____

_____

I am like HeR because I also _____

_____

But we aRe veRy diffeRent iN tHe way we _____

_____

THe way I wisH I could be moRe like HeR _____

_____

A ROLLER COASTER RIDE

If [a man] stumbles, he will not fall,
because the Lord holds his hand.

PSALM 37:24

Do you think roller coasters are awesome or awful? It seems crazy to step inside a metal car that shoots across a narrow track at insane angles and heights. What's the attraction? The thrill!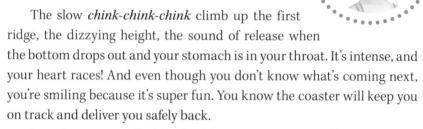

The slow *chink-chink-chink* climb up the first ridge, the dizzying height, the sound of release when the bottom drops out and your stomach is in your throat. It's intense, and your heart races! And even though you don't know what's coming next, you're smiling because it's super fun. You know the coaster will keep you on track and deliver you safely back.

Learning to trust God is a lot like stepping into a roller coaster car. Following Him and giving Him full control of your life can feel scary. But you can risk taking that adventure because God will hold you firmly through all the twists and turns of life. When you realize every moment is under His control, you can enjoy the ride and lift up your hands in delight, knowing He'll deliver you safely to your destination.

A BRAVE GIRL'S PRAYER

God, help me to be brave enough to live this
life of adventurous faith with You!

GET YOUR ARMOR ON!

You need to get God's full armor.

EPHESIANS 6:13

Read Ephesians 6:10-18. Why do we need the armor of God?

_____

List the six pieces of God's armor and how they protect you.

1. _____

2. _____

3. _____

4. _____

5. _____

6. _____

Verse eighteen is all about prayer. Why do you think it's so important

to pray? _____

_____

_____

_____

_____

_____

DRESSED FOR BATTLE

Draw a picture of yourself wearing the armor of God. Or put on things from your closet that represent each piece of God's armor, and take a selfie.

BEAUTIFULLY BRAVE

He has made everything beautiful in its time.

ECCLESIASTES 3:11 NKJV

What do you think it takes to be beautiful? Flawless skin, long eyelashes, lots of makeup, or the latest style of clothes? That's probably what you think if you get your ideas of beauty from movies and magazines. But God has a completely different perspective.

God intends for all of His girls to be gorgeous, but not with makeup or the latest clothes. In fact, He says we don't need to bother with all that stuff, because it only covers the surface. True beauty only comes from God's Spirit living inside us.

True beauty is being nice to someone who's been unkind to you, or helping your brother clean his room. It's sticking up for a kid who's being bullied or making peace between two fussing friends. In other words, true beauty comes from bravely allowing God's Spirit to work through you! When you let God's Spirit be your guide, He makes you so beautifully brave that others can't help but see His goodness through the things you do and say.

A BRAVE GIRL'S PRAYER

I want to be Your kind of beautiful, Lord. Please help me grow in Your goodness!

PRAYING POWER

Early the next morning, Jesus woke and left the house while it was still dark. He went to a place to be alone and pray.

MARK 1:35

If God already knows what's going to happen, why pray? Pick your best guess from this list:

God tells us to do it.

God's peace fills us when we do it.

Being still helps us remember who God is.

God is with us when we pray together.

God listens when we pray.

We grow closer to God when we pray.

Prayer changes things.

Did you choose them all? You should! Prayer is an extremely powerful weapon God has given you to fight off the enemy, to starve your fears, and to feed on His incredible goodness. So set aside time each day just for talking to God. During that time, use the ACTS tool to help you think of things to tell God:

A — adore and praise Him

C — confess any sins

T — tell Him everything you're thankful for

S — supplication, a fancy word for asking for what you need

A BRAVE GIRL'S PRAYER

God, I'm so glad I can talk to You about anything, whenever I need to!

A PLACE TO PRAY

We can come to God with no doubts. This means that when we ask God for things (and those things agree with what God wants for us), then God cares about what we say.

1 JOHN 5:14

Prayer is simply talking to God—so there's no right or wrong way to do it. How do you like to pray? Eyes open or closed? Sitting, standing, or walking? Head bowed or arms open wide? And where do you like to pray? God can hear you, no matter where you are! How do you pray?

_____

_____

_____

_____

If you don't have a prayer place, create one that's all your own. Find a comfy chair, dark closet, or even a spot in your room. Make sure it's somewhere peaceful and private. Gather pillows to make it snuggly. Decorate it with drawings of your favorite verses. Where can you create a prayer place?

_____

_____

_____

BATTLE TRAINING

God did not give us a spirit that makes us afraid. He
gave us a spirit of power and love and self-control.

2 TIMOTHY 1:7

Have you ever felt so fidgety you thought you might fall out of your seat? Maybe you were sitting in class for too long, or stuck inside visiting with relatives when you wanted to go outside and play instead. Sometimes it feels as if your body is telling you what to do. Instead of sitting and listening, you feel like running and talking. Instead of working, you feel like playing. So which side of you wins?

If you're listening to God's Spirit, the self-controlled side will win. Self-control is exactly what it sounds like: controlling your mind and body to make them obedient to God.

Why does it even matter? Because as children and soldiers of God, we're in a lifelong battle against evil and sin. In order to fight effectively in that battle, we must train ourselves to follow God. Part of that training is learning self-control and refusing to cave in to every thought or desire we have. Let's start with the small things so that we'll know how to stand strong when the bigger temptations roll around.

A BRAVE GIRL'S PRAYER

Lord, sometimes it's so difficult to control my
thoughts and actions. Send Your Spirit to give me
wisdom and strength to do the right thing.

MENTAL MUSCLES

I have taken your words to heart so
I would not sin against you.

PSALM 119:11

If a snake crawled up and tried to convince you to disobey God, would you listen? After freaking out, saying no would probably be easy. Although Satan doesn't sneak up on people in serpent form anymore, he does try to trip up God's people with his lies.

So how can we stay on track with what's true? God's Word! The Bible still packs amazing power for today's world. So gear up for the devil's war games by learning God's truth first. Here's the plan of attack:

❏ Choose to memorize an entire passage of Scripture or book of the Bible, one verse at a time.

❏ If you have a smartphone or tablet, download apps that give you new verses to memorize each week, plus quizzes and songs to help you remember the verses.

Over time, your mind will be strengthened by knowing God's truth. When the enemy tries to trick you, God's Spirit will help you remember what you've learned and answer evil just like Jesus did—with God's own words of truth.

A BRAVE GIRL'S PRAYER

God, help me to commit Your Word to memory
and always to turn to it for guidance.

MY FITNESS PLAN

Your body is a temple for the Holy
Spirit. The Holy Spirit is in you.

1 CORINTHIANS 6:19

Your body is an amazing gift from God, so it's important to take care of it. Whether you jump out of bed in the morning eager to exercise or you think lifting your pencil for homework counts as a workout, you can find ways to get moving all throughout your day. Maybe it's taking the stairs instead of the elevator, or shooting some hoops instead of video game aliens. Use this page to write out your fitness plan.

To get more exercise, every day I will . . .

1. _____

2. _____

At least once a week, I will . . .

1. _____

2. _____

My fitness goal is . . .

1. _____

2. _____

MY SPIRITUAL FITNESS PLAN

The Lord stayed with me. He gave me strength.

2 TIMOTHY 4:17

Just as it's important to have a physical fitness plan, it's also important to have a spiritual fitness plan. After all, you know the devil is on the prowl! Be brave by being ready for the battle!

I will read _____

_____

_____

I will pray _____

_____

_____

I will memorize _____

_____

_____

My spiritual fitness goal is _____

_____

_____

Take a Risk

Always be ready to answer everyone who asks
you to explain about the hope you have.

1 PETER 3:15

Priscilla and Aquila had listened to Paul preach about the gospel. They even had to flee from their home in Rome because of their Jewish heritage (Acts 18:2). Through all the training and trials, they came to know God and His ways very well.

So when a man named Apollos began teaching about Jesus, Priscilla and Aquila listened closely. Even though Apollos was very educated, he didn't know the full truth about how Jesus had come to save people. So Priscilla and Aquila taught Apollos all about Jesus so he could preach the gospel in the right way (Acts 18:24–28).

Priscilla and Aquila took a risk. After all, Apollos could have rejected their offer to help him or refused to believe what they had to say. But they bravely reached out to him anyway and told him the truth about Jesus. What about you? Do you have friends who need to hear about Jesus? Have you ever asked them what they believe? Learn from Priscilla and Aquila. Be bold and brave. Share the good news of Jesus!

A Brave Girl's Prayer

God, please help me be brave like Priscilla and
Aquilla. Help me share the good news of Jesus.

GIVE IT A TRY!

"I will guide them along paths they have not known.
I will make the darkness become light for them."

ISAIAH 42:16

Sometimes being brave is as simple as trying something new. Make a list of some new things you can try. For example, if you always read fiction, try a biography. If you always watch comedies, try an action movie. Go on . . . give something new a try!

A new food _____

_____

A new kind of book _____

_____

A new kind of movie _____

_____

A new hobby _____

_____

A new sport or exercise _____

_____

A new way to tell others about God _____

_____

THE GREATEST ADVENTURE

What has been the greatest adventure of your life so far?

_____

_____

_____

_____

_____

_____

_____

_____

_____

_____

ADVENTURES AHEAD!

With God's power working in us, God can do much,
much more than anything we can ask or think of.

EPHESIANS 3:20

Make a list of the adventures you would like to have someday—places
to go, things to do and see. _____

_____

_____

_____

_____

_____

What about adventures with God . . . what kind of adventures would
you like to have with Him? _____

_____

_____

_____

_____

_____

_____

Taking Courage

> "Be strong and brave. . . . The Lord your God
> will be with you everywhere you go."
>
> JOSHUA 1:9

Joshua was facing some seriously scary stuff. Moses, Israel's trusted leader, had died. Now Joshua was supposed to lead the Israelites into the Promised Land, where many more people lived—people who hated the Israelites.

God reminded Joshua, "It doesn't matter what you face, I will give you the power to overcome when you follow Me." In other words, when we are on God's side, we can't fail. We can be courageous and confident because we know He is our faithful Leader who never fails.

What would it look like for you to be strong and courageous? Maybe you'll trust God to help you tackle the new trick in gymnastics that you have feared. Perhaps it's time you told your friends at school about Jesus. Maybe it's something else.

One way to be courageous like Joshua is to read about other believers who lived boldly for Christ. (Check out the list on the next page.) You can learn from their examples, and ask the Lord to strengthen you in the same way. Because you can be brave too.

A BRAVE GIRL'S PRAYER

Jesus, I can be strong and courageous because
I know You're always with me.

COURAGEOUS FOR CHRIST

All of these men and women showed amazing strength and courage in their commitment to Jesus. Pick one, and ask your parents to help you find a library book or information online about this person. Then answer the questions that follow.

Corrie Ten Boom

Jim and Elisabeth Elliot

Eric Liddell

Amy Carmichael

Billy Graham

George Mueller

Florence Nightingale

C. S. Lewis

Martin Luther King Jr.

Bruce Olsen

What did this person do that was strong and courageous? _____

_____

_____

How did God help him or her? _____

_____

_____

How can this person's story help you to be strong and courageous too?

_____

_____

DO WHAT YOU CAN DO

"THIS woman did the only thing she could do for me. She poured perfume on my body. She did this before I die to prepare me for burial."

MARK 14:8

Jesus has done so many amazing things, the woman thought. *He has stilled storms. He has healed the blind and the sick, and He has raised people from the dead. He has even taken away my sins. What can I possibly do for Him?*

What that long-ago woman did was break open a bottle of perfume and pour it over Him. She couldn't stop the Pharisees from hating Him, and she couldn't stop Him from going to the cross. But she could love Him and worship Him. So she did what she could do.

The Lord has done so much for you too. He's loved you, cared for you, and taken away your sins. What can you do for Him? You can love Him, and You can worship Him—for all the world to see. You can praise Him for who He is and for all that He has done. So be brave, and go and do what you can do! God's going to love it.

A BRAVE GIRL'S PRAYER

Lord, I want to live my life praising You. Thank You for all You do for me each and every day.

what can you do?

The woman from Mark 14:3–9 bravely chose to worship Jesus in front of many people, even those who hated Him. Read her story.

Why was what she did so brave? _____

_____

_____

_____

Why did Jesus say that what she did was beautiful? _____

_____

_____

_____

Whether it's big and bold, or small and simple, what can you do to show the world you love Jesus? _____

_____

_____

NOTHING BIGGER

WHO HAS MEASURED THE OCEANS IN THE PALM OF HIS
HAND? WHO HAS USED HIS HAND TO MEASURE THE SKY?

ISAIAH 40:12

What's the biggest thing you can think of? A mountain? The Grand Canyon? The moon? No matter what you can think of, there's one thing that's bigger—God! He's bigger than anything because He created everything. He can hold the whole ocean in the palm of His hand. He can measure the sky with His fingers. God is so big that He knows every star and can count every grain of sand.

God is bigger than we could ever imagine—and more powerful too. That means there's no problem bigger than Him and no trouble too tough for Him. But the very best thing about God isn't how big or how strong or how mighty He is; it's how much He loves each and every one of us. His love for us is bigger than any ocean and stretches even farther than the sky. It's so big that He sacrificed His Son to save us. So let's be brave! Because there's nothing bigger than our God and His love for us !

A BRAVE GIRL'S PRAYER

Lord, You are so big and so mighty, but You still love someone as small as me. Thank You, God, for making me feel big and brave with Your love.

SEEING GOD

The heavens tell the glory of God. And the
skies announce what his hands have made. Day
after day they tell the story. Night after
night they tell it again. They have no speech
or words. They don't make any sound to be
heard. But their message goes out through all
the world. It goes everywhere on earth.

PSALM 19:1–4

These verses, Psalm 19:1-4, tell me that God is _____

_____

Though I can't see God face to face right now, I feel closest to Him when

_____

I know God is with me when _____

_____

The thing that amazes me most about God's creation is _____

_____

I am reminded that God is always with me when I see _____

_____

I feel God's presence and power when I see _____

_____

SMALL WONDER

"WHEN you are weak, THEN my power
is made perfect in you."

2 CORINTHIANS 12:9

At first glance, the hummingbird looks like a fragile bird because it is impossibly small with a very long beak. But did you know that hummingbirds have an amazing memory? They can remember each flower they've visited and how long it will take for that flower's nectar to refill. And when a hummingbird takes flight, its wings flap so fast you can't even see them move. While they're zipping, diving, hovering, and even flying backward, it's easy to see that God packed a lot into this tiny package.

God does the same thing with you. It doesn't matter if you feel too young or small to make a difference in your world. God has packed you with amazing power and skill—coming from His own Spirit in you! Just as a hummingbird looks for flowers, you are to look for people who need God's love. Don't worry or be afraid! God will give you everything you need to spread the joy of His love, making the world a more beautiful place.

A BRAVE GIRL'S PRAYER

Thank You, Lord, for Your grace and power working in me. Help me to be strong and able to do Your work.

WEAK OR STRONG?

When I am weak, then I am truly strong.

2 CORINTHIANS 12:10

What does the word **weakness** mean to you? _____

_____

What about **strength**? What does it mean to you? _____

_____

Write out a prayer and ask God to show you your weaknesses and help

you to be strong. _____

_____

_____

_____

_____

_____

_____

_____

_____

_____

Safe and Secure

God Has said, "I will NeveR leave you;
I will NeveR abandon you."

HEBREWS 13:5

Have you ever gotten lost in a store? One minute you were exploring all the new clothes, feeling safe and fine. But the next minute, you were all alone—and all those good feelings vanished. Panic set in as you wandered up and down aisles, hoping to find your mom or dad so you could feel safe again.

Sometimes we feel that way even when we aren't lost. Facing hard times—like sickness, death, or divorce—can cause that same lost and lonely feeling. Jesus' followers felt that way when He was crucified, and again when He rose up into heaven.

But Jesus didn't want them to feel alone, and He doesn't want us to either. He promised never to leave us—and He doesn't! When we follow Him, He puts His Spirit inside us. So no matter where we go, Jesus is right there with us. Feelings of loneliness and sadness are signals for us to stop and remember that He is with us, helping us to be strong and brave—even if we can't see Him.

A BRAVe GIRL'S PRAYeR

Jesus, tHank You foR always being witH me—now and foRever.

WHO YOU REALLY ARE

"You are precious to me . . . and I love you."

ISAIAH 43:4

Want to know who God says you really are? Take a look at these verses. Match each verse to the words God uses to describe you.

Ephesians 1:4	friend of Jesus
Ephesians 2:10	child of God
Philippians 3:20	forgiven
1 Corinthians 6:19	made by God
Matthew 5:14	chosen
1 John 1:9	holy, chosen, and blameless
John 1:12	the light of the world
Psalm 139:14	a temple of the Holy Spirit
1 Peter 2:9	a citizen of heaven

THE INVISIBLE GIRL

The slave girl gave a name to the Lord who spoke to
her. She said to Him, "You are 'God who sees me.'"

GENESIS 16:13

Megan stood by her locker watching all the other girls laughing and talking around her. They were talking about a big slumber party one of the girls was having. Megan wasn't invited. She tried not to let the girls see that she was upset, but it probably didn't matter anyway. They didn't even notice her—it was like she was invisible.

Have you ever felt invisible like Megan? Some people can leave us feeling unwanted, unimportant, and completely invisible. But that's not true. God sees you. And this is what He says about you:

- "Everything about you is beautiful. There is nothing at all wrong with you" (Song of Solomon 4:7).

- God "even knows how many hairs you have on your head" (Luke 12:7).

- God has "written your name on [His] hand" (Isaiah 49:16).

- "He will not leave you or forget you" (Deuteronomy 31:8).

You're never invisible to God, never unwanted or unimportant. You are His beloved child. So stand tall and be brave—because He always sees you!

A BRAVE GIRL'S PRAYER

Lord, when I feel invisible, help me to remember
You always see me and love me.

YOU ARE KNOWN

Lord, you have examined me. You know all about me.

PSALM 139:1

God can give you everything you need to do His will. He can even help you be brave! God is able to do that because He knows you perfectly—from the inside out. After all, He created you!

Read Psalm 139 to discover just how well God knows you and how special you are to Him. Then fill in the blanks to the verses below (use the International Children's Bible translation) and complete the crossword puzzle.

Across

1. God knows my _____ before I think them.
2. God's knowledge about me is more than I can _____.
3. Where can I go to get away from your Spirit? _____.
4. You promise to hold me with Your _____.

Down

1. God _____ me in my mother's body.
2. God says His work in me is amazing and _____.
3. God says all my days were _____ for me.
4. If I tried to count all the times God thinks about me, they would outnumber the _____.

Answers: Across—1. thoughts; 2. understand; 3. nowhere; 4. right hand
Down—1. formed; 2. wonderful; 3. planned; 4. grains of sand

COLORFUL IMPACT

You are young, but do not let anyone treat
you as if you were not important.

1 TIMOTHY 4:12

Have you ever seen a male peacock fanning his tail feathers to show off his rainbow of colors? Now picture all those brilliant colors poured onto a shrimp. Sound impossible? Not for the peacock mantis shrimp. Not only is it colorful, but it has two eyes that can see ten times more color than ours can. Oh, and another thing—these little guys are fast. They can propel through the water at speeds so fast your eyes can hardly see them, causing deadly damage to the crabs or mollusks they are hunting.

So what would the peacock mantis shrimp tell you (if it could)? Don't worry about your size or shape or age. God designed you to bring beauty, color, and brilliant energy into the world just by being you and doing what you do. When you love God and bravely trust the direction He has for your life, you're bound to have tremendous impact as He propels you to bring life and love to everyone around you.

A BRAVE GIRL'S PRAYER

Lord, thank You for using someone small
like me to do big things for You.

I can Do THaT!

Remember to use the gift that you have.

1 TIMOTHY 4:14

List three things you can do really well.

1. _____

2. _____

3. _____

How can you use those talents to help you to be brave? (For example, if you're good at baking, perhaps sharing a warm batch of cookies or a cake could help you make new friends or comfort someone.)

1. _____

2. _____

3. _____

4. _____

5. _____

6. _____

GOD'S GOT THIS

All the days planned for me were written
in your book before I was one day old.

PSALM 139:16

Are you a planner? Lots of people are. They plan what to wear, what to do, what to say. Plans can make us feel more comfortable and in control of what's happening around us.

But no matter how carefully we plan, there'll be times when life doesn't go according to our plans. Maybe it's something small like a rip in your favorite jeans, or something bigger like a pop quiz. Or maybe it's something really big like a move, an accident, or someone in your family getting sick. Whatever it is, it's thrown your plans all out of whack, and now you're not quite sure what to do.

Well, first, stop worrying. Be brave and remember that God's got this. Seriously, that thing that surprised you didn't surprise Him at all. In fact, He's had a plan to take care of this since before you were even born. So just relax and trust God—because He's got this.

A BRAVE GIRL'S PRAYER

Lord, my plans have gotten all messed up, but I
know You've got this. I won't worry. Instead, I'll
trust You because You know just what to do.

PLAN FOR BRAVERY!

Depend on the Lord in whatever you
do. Then your plans will succeed.

PROVERBS 16:3

MAKE YOUR VERY OWN BRAVE GIRL CALENDAR!

Ask your mom or dad to help you print out a blank calendar page (or draw
one of your own). Fill in each day with an idea for reaching out to others,
a reminder that God is in control, and a verse that helps you feel brave.

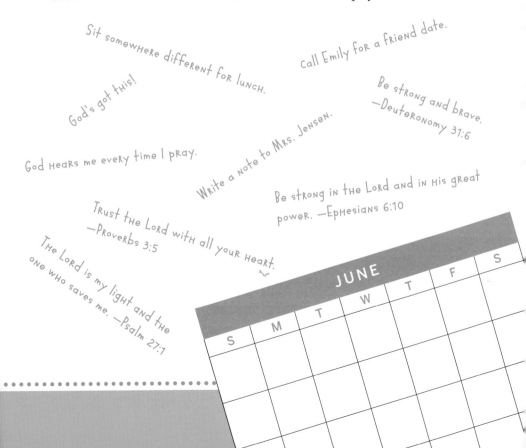

Sit somewhere different for lunch.

Call Emily for a friend date.

God's got this!

Be strong and brave.
—Deuteronomy 31:6

God hears me every time I pray.

Write a note to Mrs. Jensen.

Be strong in the Lord and in His great
power. —Ephesians 6:10

Trust the Lord with all your heart.
—Proverbs 3:5

The Lord is my light and the
one who saves me. —Psalm 27:1

JUNE

S M T W T F S

A CUT ABOVE

"They shall be Mine," says the Lord of hosts,
"on the day that I make them My jewels."

MALACHI 3:17 NKJV

Have you ever visited a jewelry store? Glass cases are filled with gems, each one specially cut and set in rings, earrings, bracelets, and necklaces to add beauty and color to the person who gets to wear them. Since almost the beginning of time, people have recognized certain gems—like diamonds, rubies, emeralds, and sapphires—as rare and precious. Though they come out of the ground looking rough and cloudy, these special gems are cut just the right way to reveal the incredible beauty within.

Did you know that God views you as a precious jewel? Though you may not always see the beauty of your soul, God does. He has formed you and filled you with His own Spirit so that your life will sparkle with His light and love. Just as gems must be cut to reveal their deepest beauty, God works through the difficult times in your life to shape your character. When times get rough or scary, be brave and trust Him. God is using every moment in your life—even the toughest ones—to transform you into a beautiful gem!

A BRAVE GIRL'S PRAYER

Thank You, Jesus, for seeing me as beautiful
to You and valuable to Your world.

THE POTTER'S HANDS

Lord, you are our Father. We are like clay, and
you are the potter. Your hands made us all.

ISAIAH 64:8

Have you ever worked with clay on a potter's wheel? First, you place your lump of clay on the center of the wheel. Then you gently press into the center of it as the wheel turns, using your fingers to gradually shape a bowl, a cup, or a vase.

God says that people are like clay, and He is the Potter. Just as He formed Adam from the dust of the ground, He shapes who we are. He presses in—using the people in our lives and our experiences, both good and bad—to mold us and make us fit for the purpose He has planned for us. We might not always like the molding and shaping part—and it may take a little courage (or a lot!) to trust God's design for us. But we can believe God knows exactly what He's doing.

Your life is safe in God's hands. Instead of fighting the way He is shaping you, open your eyes and heart to His plans for you—they'll always be perfectly designed.

A BRAVE GIRL'S PRAYER

Father, I trust You to use every moment in my life
to shape me into the person You want me to be.

GOD'S FINGERPRINTS

"You are like the clay in the potter's hands."

JEREMIAH 18:6

What you need:

- air-dry clay
- magnifying glass

Directions:

Grab a chunk of air-dry clay and shape it into anything you want—a bowl, a vase, a chewing gum holder—whatever you'd like. Before you set your creation aside to harden, use your magnifying glass and take an up-close look. What do you see? Your fingerprints!

Now think about Isaiah 64:8:

Lord, you are our father.
We are like clay, and you are the potter.
Your hands made us all.

If you are like the clay and God is the One who shapes you, then whose fingerprints are all over you? _____

_____

_____

_____

What does that tell you about the way you are made? _____

_____

_____

_____

_____

_____

_____

_____

_____

WHEN IT COMES TO MYSELF . . .

I love . . . _____

_____

_____

_____

I wish I could change . . . _____

_____

_____

_____

I want . . . _____

_____

_____

_____

I hope . . . _____

_____

_____

_____

I believe . . . _____

_____

_____

_____

I pRay . . . _____

_____

_____

_____

_____

WHEN IT COMES TO
MY FRIENDS . . .

I love . . . _____

_____

_____

_____

I wish I could change . . . _____

_____

_____

_____

I want . . . _____

_____

_____

_____

I hope . . . _____

_____

_____

_____

I believe . . . _____

_____

_____

_____

I pRay . . . _____

_____

_____

_____

_____

_____

_____

_____

WHEN IT COMES TO MY FAMILY . . .

I love . . . _____

_____

_____

_____

I wish I could change . . . _____

_____

_____

_____

I want . . . _____

_____

_____

_____

I hope . . . _____

_____

_____

_____

I believe . . . _____

_____

_____

_____

I pRAy . . . _____

_____

_____

_____

_____

WHEN IT COMES TO ME AND GOD . . .

I love . . . _____

_____

_____

_____

I wish I could change . . . _____

_____

_____

_____

I want . . . _____

_____

_____

_____

I hope . . . _____

_____

_____

_____

I believe . . . _____

_____

_____

_____

I pRay . . . _____

_____

_____

_____

_____

SHINING STARS

You are living with crooked and mean
people all around you. Among them you
shine like stars in the dark world. You offer
to them the teaching that gives life.

PHILIPPIANS 2:15–16

If you take a trip out into the country, past where the streetlights end, you'll be able to see the heavens stretching overhead like a dark, velvet blanket dotted with brilliant sparkles of light. Individually, each star is only a tiny light in the great big darkness. But together, they brighten up the whole night sky, shining all the way down to earth.

God says that believers are just like those shining stars. Lit up by God's Spirit inside us, we have been forgiven, saved, and honored by God. And we have love to give because we have been loved first. As we show others what it means to know Jesus, His light shines out of us, pierces the darkness of this world, and draws other people to Him. So be brave . . . shine the light of Jesus for all the world to see.

A BRAVE GIRL'S PRAYER

Father, thank You for filling me with Your light
to give lasting joy to others around me.

LIGHT UP THE WORLD

"You are the light that gives light to the world."

MATTHEW 5:14

As children of God, our lives look very different from the dark world around us. The Bible calls people who do not believe in God "lost" because they cannot find a lasting purpose or meaning in life. When people look to the things of the world for happiness, they will always be disappointed—never finding joy, peace, or true life. Can you think of some things people look to for happiness instead of God?

_____

_____

_____

When you belong to God, you have the light of Jesus' hope. How does following Jesus help you to shine in this dark world?

_____

_____

_____

_____

_____

LEAVING THE COMFORT ZONE

"And the second command is like the first:
'Love your neighbor as you love yourself.'"

MATTHEW 22:39

"Who is my neighbor?" a man asked, and Jesus told him of a Jewish man who was robbed, beaten, and left for dead along the roadside. A priest and a temple worker passed by, but they did not stop to help. Then a Samaritan (part of a nation the Jews hated) saw the man and helped him. Who was that man's neighbor? The Samaritan who had helped him. Then Jesus said, "Go and do the same" (Luke 10:25–37).

To Jesus a neighbor isn't just someone who lives next door. A neighbor is anyone in need. It could be the person who lives across town, across the world, or even inside your own house. How can you be a good neighbor to everyone? Be brave, and step out of your comfort zone. Think of one idea to help each person, and try them out this week.

The neighbor next door _____

The neighbor across town _____

The neighbor across the world _____

The neighbor inside my house _____

A BRAVE GIRL'S PRAYER

Lord, help me be a good neighbor to everyone I meet.

CULTIVATING CULTURES

Do not be interested only in your own life,
but be interested in the lives of others.

PHILIPPIANS 2:4

Reaching out to people from another culture often requires a bit of bravery. And it definitely requires respect. Pick a restaurant or perhaps a festival from another culture, and give it a try. Notice not only the kinds of foods they like to eat, but also the music, the colors, the decorations, and the language the people use.

What did you observe? _____

_____

Did you enjoy the food? The music? The decorations? _____

_____

How were you alike? _____

_____

How were you different? _____

_____

How would this help you talk to someone from that culture? _____

_____

_____

IF I COULD . . .

No one has ever imagined what God has prepared for those who love Him.

1 CORINTHIANS 2:9

If I could travel anywhere, it would be _____

If I could be anything, it would be _____

If I could do anything, it would be _____

If I could have anything, it would be _____

If I could live during any time, it would be _____

If I could talk to anyone over a slice of pizza, it would be _____

If I could be teacher for a day, I would _____

If I knew I couldn't possibly fail, I would _____

If I knew no one would laugh, I would _____

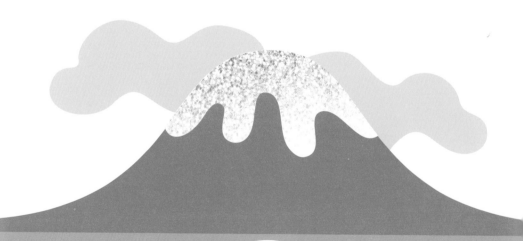

LOVING THE LEAST

"Take care of the needs of those who are troubled.
Then your light will shine in the darkness."

ISAIAH 58:10

Have you ever had a cold or the flu? People probably didn't want to get too close to you. Back in Jesus' day, the Jews didn't want to be around sick or disabled people either. They were afraid they might "catch" whatever those people had. So for those with long-lasting illnesses, like leprosy, life was miserable. Not only were they sick, but people avoided them and acted as if they were cursed.

When Jesus began His ministry, He didn't avoid the poor and sick; He touched and healed them. He never saw some people as better than others. They were all like lost sheep who needed Him, the Good Shepherd.

When you look at people, what do you see? Are you drawn more to those who look good and are popular? Do you avoid those who don't fit in? Ask Jesus to help you see His beauty in everyone you meet. Then ask Him to make you brave enough to love both the greatest and the least with all your heart.

A BRAVE GIRL'S PRAYER

Lord, help me see the beauty and value
in everyone You've made.

ICEBREAKERS

The Lord sees the good people. He listens
to their prayers. . . . The Lord hears
good people when they cry out to Him. He
saves them from all their troubles.

PSALM 34:15, 17

Do you remember the first time you ever met your best friend? Chances are the first conversation was a bit awkward. But the more you two talked, the more you found in common with each other. And now you're as comfortable with your best friend as you are with anyone in your family.

The same is true when you are hanging out with God. At first, it might seem really weird to talk to someone you can't see. Many kids *and* adults wonder, *What should I say?* Or, *How does this work?* And, *What if I mess up?*

But relax! Don't be afraid! God is super interested in whatever you have to say. You will be surprised how quickly you become comfortable telling Him whatever's on your mind. Soon, you'll be talking out loud or in your heart all day long and including your new Best Friend in everything you do.

A BRAVE GIRL'S PRAYER

God, thank You for always listening to what I say.
Remind me always to come to You with my thoughts.

WHATEVER YOU NEED

"Say the things God gives you to say
at that time. It will not really be you
speaking. It will be the Holy Spirit."

MARK 13:11

Do you like to talk in front of crowds? Moses didn't. But when he met God at the burning bush, God gave Moses a clear command: "Go to Egypt and tell Pharaoh to let My people go."

Gulp! Moses didn't want to go back to Egypt. (He had killed an Egyptian years ago, and Pharaoh wanted him dead.) He especially didn't want to tell Pharaoh to let God's people go.

Yet that's what God wanted Moses to do. And God promised to help Moses in his weakness. He even allowed Aaron, Moses' brother, to come alongside and speak for him. And God used them both to defeat Pharaoh and free His people. (Read about Moses in Exodus 3–14.)

So what do you think your greatest weaknesses are? Remember Moses' story, and know that the God who helped Moses helps you too. You can be brave because God will give you everything you need to succeed in whatever He calls you to do.

A BRAVE GIRL'S PRAYER

Father, when I am weak, You are strong.
Give me the strength to obey You.

EXCUSES, EXCUSES

Moses said, "Please, Lord, send someone else."
The Lord became angry with Moses.

EXODUS 4:13–14

Do you ever make up excuses for not being brave? Moses sure did! Check out all his excuses in the story of the burning bush in Exodus 3:1–4:17.

How many reasons did Moses give for not obeying God? _____

_____

What did God do for every excuse? _____

_____

Do you ever make up excuses for not trying new things, meeting new people, or even following God? _____

_____

Do you make excuses for any of the following?

- putting off my homework
- not doing my chores
- not following God
- not telling others about God

What do you think God would have to say about your excuses?

_____

_____

MISSION FIELDS

"There are many people to harvest, but there are only a few workers to help harvest them."

MATTHEW 9:37

When you think of the mission field, what comes to mind? Dirt roads, palm trees, and people who don't speak your language? For sure, some mission fields look like that. But guess what? Right where you live is a mission field too.

Try one of these activities to help you connect with your neighbors and show them God's love!

- Bake cookies, put them in a container, and include a card that says, "God loves you, and I do too!" Take them over to your neighbor's house. Share that you are praying for the people in your neighborhood and ask how you can pray for them.

- Offer to mow your neighbor's grass, rake their leaves, or take their. Tell them you want to serve people like Jesus did.

- Start a Backyard Bible Club with your friends. Meet once a week to pray and work on projects to help others.

A BRAVE GIRL'S PRAYER

Jesus, please use me to help my neighbors know Your love better.

LOSE THE LONELINESS

Turn to me and be kind to me.
I am lonely and hurting.

PSALM 25:16

SCENARIO

It wasn't that she didn't have *any* friends. Bella knew there were plenty of people she could call to invite over. *But how come nobody ever invites me?* she wondered. *I guess they don't really want to be with me.*

Meanwhile, two streets down, Hadley was thinking, *I'm so lonely! Nobody ever wants to hang out with me. What's wrong with me?*

SOLUTION

Both Bella and Hadley feel alone and sad. The truth is, all people feel lonely sometimes. Because of Adam and Eve's sin, our relationships with God and each other became messed up. But God has fixed the brokenness through Jesus. Now we never have to feel alone because Jesus is always with us.

Whenever we're feeling lonely, we first need to talk to Jesus and ask Him to help us know He's there. Then we bravely need to step out and follow Jesus' example. He left heaven to come and invite us into friendship with Him, so we need to reach out to others and invite them to be our friends too.

Yes, it takes courage . . . but you can do it, brave girl!

A BRAVE GIRL'S PRAYER

Lord, loneliness is difficult, but it reminds me to talk to You and reach out to others. Thank You for being a faithful friend.

sweet treat

*"You have good news to tell. . . . Shout
it out and don't be afraid."*

ISAIAH 40:9

So your mom made her yummiest chocolate chip cookies last night, and you brought some to school. You couldn't wait to pass them around to your friends at lunch! They didn't even have to ask for a cookie because your friends know you always share good things with them.

Now think about Jesus for a minute. He is good, right? Like, *really* good. Better than chocolate chip cookies or a new video game or a vacation, or any of the other things we love to tell our friends about. So if we know that being friends with Jesus means love, joy, and everlasting peace with God, why don't we share the good news with our friends who don't know Him?

We have to admit: we're afraid our friends might think we are weird. But Jesus wants us to share what we know because it gives others a taste of God's goodness—just like that cookie. When your friends are ready, they'll be glad you were willing to share the sweet treat of knowing Jesus.

A BRAVE GIRL'S PRAYER

Jesus, make me brave to share Your love
and truth with my friends.

FRIENDSHIP POSSIBILITIES

Let us think about each other and help each
other to show love and do good deeds.

HEBREWS 10:24

Friendship is a gift that grows greater each time you give it. So make a list of at least five people you can offer the gift of friendship to. Try to include someone who is often left out, someone from a different country or culture, and someone you wouldn't usually be friends with. Under each name, write one way you can reach out in friendship.

1. Name _____ I can be a friend by _____

_____

2. Name _____ I can be a friend by _____

_____

3. Name _____ I can be a friend by _____

_____

4. Name _____ I can be a friend by _____

_____

5. Name _____ I can be a friend by _____

_____

LUNCH RULES

WHEN you talk, you should always be kind
and wise. THEN you will be able to answer
everyone in the way you should.

COLOSSIANS 4:6

For some, lunch is a nice break from class and a time to catch up with friends. But for others, it can be the most stressful part of the day. The *Whom will I sit with?* and *What will I say?* questions can really ruin your appetite. But no need to stress. Be brave—and come prepared with these simple conversation tips, and lunchtime will go down easier than ice cream!

- Try to sit toward the middle of the table so you'll have people on all sides to chat with.

- Say hi to the people around you, making sure to use their names.

- Ask questions that will require them to answer, like, "How's the food today?" or, "Did anybody watch _____ last night?"

- Based on their answer, ask a follow-up question that will get them to talk more. (For example, "What did you think of how it ended?")

- Volunteer information about yourself, such as, "I went shopping yesterday," or, "I won my soccer game last night." Wait to see if anyone asks you questions about it. If not, offer a few more details. Then change topics if no one seems interested.

- Keep the conversation clean and God-honoring.

A BRAVE GIRL'S PRAYER

Lord, help me be bold when approaching new faces, and give me courage to make new friends.

OUT OF THE BOX

Where God's love is, there is no fear, because
God's perfect love takes away fear.

1 JOHN 4:18

Every day you go to school, you follow the same routine. You know what to expect, and that's great—schedules and order make our world feel safer and easier to handle.

But God hasn't called us to feel comfortable all the time. Instead, He wants us to grow in our obedience and trust in His Spirit, and sometimes that means getting out of our comfort zone. That can feel scary, but remember: God can make us brave!

Consider the ideas below and pray about them, asking God if He'd like you to try them. Then ask for the power and bravery to obey!

- Invite someone new to sit with you at lunch.

- Look for the quiet person who rarely talks in class, and strike up a conversation with her.

- In gym class, choose kids who are usually picked last to be on your team.

- Try a new way of serving God—even if it isn't considered "cool."

A BRAVE GIRL'S PRAYER

Lord, please make me brave enough to go where You
want me to go and to tell others about You.

WE'RE TALKING GROWN-UPS

The Lord said to Him, "Who made man's mouth? . . . Now go! I will help you speak. I will tell you what to say."

EXODUS 4:11–12

Sometimes you have to talk to grown-ups. Maybe you find yourself seated next to a grown-up at the dinner table. Or maybe your friend's parent is driving you home. It can be a bit scary sometimes! What on earth are you supposed to say?

Remember that adults were once kids just like you. Instead of shrinking into your seat, sit up and start a good conversation using these tips:

1. Start with something polite, such as, "How are you doing?"
2. Ask them something about themselves, such as, "What do you do when you're not driving kids around?"
3. They'll probably ask you a question in return. Answer with details. Ask a related question.

Before you know it, dinner will be over or you'll have reached your destination, and you'll have made a new friend in the process!

A BRAVE GIRL'S PRAYER

Lord, please give me courage when I'm nervous and the wisdom to connect well with others, no matter their age.

BIBLE BRAVERY

All you who put your hope in the
Lord be strong and brave.

PSALM 31:24

Out of all the brave people in the Bible, whom do you admire most?

_____

What brave thing did she or he do? _____

_____

What was something unique about her or him? _____

_____

What helped that person to be so brave? _____

_____

In what ways do you want to be more like her or him? ___

HOLY BIBLE

_____

_____

_____

_____

_____

COOL WITH KIDS

"If anyone accepts children like these in
my name, then he is also accepting me."

MARK 9:37

Does the idea of playing with little kids make you uncomfortable? Even though some people naturally seem to know how to handle children, these tricks will help you be the best babysitter in town.

- Get down on their level. Sit down with them so they can get a good look at you and you can talk to them eye to eye.

- Adjust your expectations. Little kids aren't going to talk to you like someone your own age would. Speak in shorter sentences, and use simple phrases.

- Plan a variety of activities. Little kids have very short attention spans. They won't stay on one activity for long.

- As you play, ask them simple questions about what they are doing. For example, if you are building with blocks, ask them, "Are you building a house?"

By the end of your time, you will be their new best friend. Be brave . . . and you'll learn that little kids aren't so bad after all!

A BRAVE GIRL'S PRAYER

God, please help me be a brave example to little
ones so they can bravely follow You too.

LOVE BRAVELY

"But I tell you, love your enemies.
Pray for those who hurt you."

MATTHEW 5:44

Everyone at church was concerned. Outside, a large group of atheists (people who don't believe God is real) was picketing. One of the church members barged out of the church yelling, "Go away! You and your stupid ideas aren't welcome here!" Picketers yelled back.

Then a young, brave girl decided to take action. She got her youth group to help her load up some trays of donuts and juice that were supposed to be for Sunday school. Instead, they prayed for help and wisdom, and then took the goodies outside to the picketers. As they handed out the juice and donuts, the kids smiled and told the people that God loved them and cared for them as they handed out the juice and donuts. After a while, the picketers got quiet. Eventually they all left—except for one man. He followed the kids back into the church, sat through the sermon, and gave his life to Jesus.

- Which church member was truly loving her enemies?

- How was that young girl both brave and loving?

- Why is it so important to love others well, especially those who seem like our enemies?

A BRAVE GIRL'S PRAYER

Jesus, You were so brave in showing Your love
for people. Help me to be more like You.

PaY BaCK OR BLeSS BaCK?

Do not do wrong to a person to pay
him back for doing wrong to you. . . .
But ask God to bless that person.

1 PETER 3:9

Gracie knew that going to a new school wouldn't be easy, but she could hardly believe what happened one day. "Did you hear what Tara is saying about you?" Ava, one of Gracie's new friends, asked. "She's saying you're stuck-up and people shouldn't talk to you." Tara was one of the popular girls, and Gracie became very worried.

It would be easy to lash back at Tara in anger with words like, "*She's the one who's stuck-up . . . and super snotty! She doesn't know who she's messing with. I can make life just as miserable for her.*"

But even though being kind might be risky, Gracie knew that was what God would want her to do. So she said, "Well, I guess Tara just doesn't know me yet." Then she silently prayed, *Lord, help me make good friends here, and help Tara see the truth.*

The next day, Gracie helped Tara pick up books she dropped. Tara still wasn't friendly, but Gracie said, "Hey, I can be quiet sometimes, but I'm not stuck-up. I'd really like to be friends with everyone here."

Striking back out of anger is the easy way out. But Brave Girls know God wants them to be different: bless back and don't pay back.

A BRaVE GIRL'S PRaYeR

God, help me be kind to others, even
when they are not kind to me.

TOP 10 WAYS TO BUILD UP OTHERS

So comfort each other and give each other
strength, just as you are doing now.

1 THESSALONIANS 5:11

Building up others is an important part of being a Christian. But it takes a Brave Girl to be willing to reach out to others. Check out these ten ways to comfort and help someone, and give one of them a try today.

1. Pray for God to help people come to know Him.
2. Give them a great big hug and a smile.
3. Write little notes to tell them you care, and stick them in special places where they'll find them.
4. Call to see how they are doing.
5. Text them a Bible verse that has encouraged you.
6. Invite them to join you at church.
7. Cry with them when they are sad.
8. Celebrate their birthdays, victories, and accomplishments with balloons or banners or a special food treat.
9. Ask them how you can help them or pray for them.
10. Remind them every day how much you and God love them!

What other ways can you think of to encourage the people in your life?

_____

_____

_____

_____

How have others encouraged you? _____

_____

_____

_____

_____

_____

_____

_____

THE GREAT FRIENDSHIP CHALLENGE

Do not be proud, but make friends with those who seem unimportant. Do not think how smart you are.

ROMANS 12:16

Do you know who Jesus' closest friends were? Well, they were nothing like Him. After all, Jesus was the Son of God. But His closest friends on earth were a bunch of fishermen (including Peter, Andrew, James, and John) who were respectable, but definitely not high society. There was also Matthew, a tax collector—a profession the Jews hated. Jesus hung out with the poor, the sick, sinners, and outcasts. He wasn't too proud to talk to anyone, and He never made anyone feel unimportant.

Can you say the same about yourself? Or do you only hang out with people who are pretty much like you? Today, be brave. Step out of your friendship comfort zone and take the Great Friendship Challenge. Talk to at least three kids you don't usually talk to. Invite a new person to join your group. And pick at least one person to try and get to know better. Who knows? You might make a new friend.

A BRAVE GIRL'S PRAYER

Lord, I want to be a friend to everyone, just like Jesus was. Please give me the courage to make new friends.

RIPPING UP THE ROOF

THey went to the roof above Jesus and made a hole in the roof. THen they lowered the mat with the paralyzed man on it.

MARK 2:4

Four men were bringing their friend to see Jesus. Their friend was paralyzed, so they carried him on a mat. But when they came to the place where Jesus was, it was so crowded that they couldn't get in. Then they had an idea.

The four men climbed up on the roof and began tearing into it! They ripped and dug and pulled until they'd made a hole big enough for their friend. Then they lowered him down to Jesus—and he was healed. Nothing could stop these four friends from bringing their friend to Jesus. Not even a roof!

Would you do anything to bring your friends to Jesus? Would you risk being embarrassed, or made fun of, or just told no? Jesus wants you to tell others about Him. So be brave! Bring your friends to Jesus—whatever it takes!

A BRAVE GIRL'S PRAYER

Jesus, I have friends who do not know You. Show me how I can bring them to You—and then help me be brave enough to do it.

RIP IT UP!

Come near to God, and God will come near to you.

JAMES 4:8

Those friends in Mark 2:1–17 were willing to rip up a roof in order to bring their friend to Jesus. What are you willing to "rip up" to bring your friends to Jesus? _____

_____

_____

_____

_____

What do you need to "rip up" to bring yourself closer to Jesus?

_____

_____

_____

_____

_____

WITH ALL YOU'VE GOT

"Love the Lord your God with all
your heart, soul and mind."

MATTHEW 22:37

What does *love* mean to you? Most people would say it's that wonderful, warm feeling we get when we're with someone we care about. But love is much more than that. Love is your mom staying up all night with you when you're sick. Love is your dad patiently helping you build a project for the science fair. Love is the friend who listens to the same joke for the tenth time—and still laughs.

Love isn't just a feeling. It's something you *do* with all you've got. And that's how God asks you to love Him—with all you've got. It's not always easy. Sometimes you'll need to be brave, especially when you're having a rough day. But loving God with all you've got means praying for peace when you're angry, singing when you're sad, and doing good things for others even if you're tired—or just tired of them.

God wants you to love Him with all that you've got and without end. Why? Because that's how He loves you—with all that He's got and without end.

A BRAVE GIRL'S PRAYER

Lord, please give me the courage and strength
to love You and others with all I've got.

BUILT FOR BRAVERY and BLESSINGS

Jesus has the power of God. His power has given us everything we need to live and to serve God.

2 PETER 1:3

Because we have God's Spirit living inside us, we have everything we need to be brave, build strong friendships, and honor God. But we have to do more than just know the truth. We have to apply it to our lives and work hard to live it out.

Search for the following words from 2 Peter 1:5–8 that describe the qualities we must seek to add to our lives as we try to live brave for God.

FAITH

GOODNESS

KNOWLEDGE

SELF-CONTROL

PERSEVERANCE

SERVICE

KINDNESS

LOVE

L	W	K	A	Z	F	D	U	E	E	S	E
W	O	Q	I	A	H	Z	Z	G	T	E	C
T	Q	R	I	N	E	D	D	W	T	R	N
T	Z	T	T	Y	D	E	V	O	L	V	A
Y	H	D	Z	N	L	N	S	N	W	I	R
Q	L	J	Q	W	O	Y	E	B	C	C	E
S	B	V	O	R	Q	C	O	S	Y	E	V
A	A	N	O	Q	X	S	F	O	S	L	E
G	K	I	Z	U	P	O	N	L	N	S	S
N	F	F	O	K	G	F	Q	H	E	P	R
G	F	N	H	H	F	S	O	H	B	S	E
G	O	O	D	N	E	S	S	V	N	T	P

STRONGER TOGETHER

Two people are better than one. . . . If one
person falls, the other can help him up.

ECCLESIASTES 4:9–10

Can you imagine what the people in Noah's day must have thought when Noah started building a gigantic boat in the middle of dry land? Everybody probably told him he was crazy.

We know those folks weren't listening to God like Noah was. And their foolishness cost them their lives. Noah's story (Genesis 6–9) reminds us that being friends with God makes a lot more sense than listening to people who don't know Him.

What about you? Are there areas in your life where you are listening to the world instead of to God? How about your choices of music, television, or movies? Do your friends help you love God? Do the way you speak to your parents and the way you spend your free time honor God?

If not, ask God to forgive you, and pray for strength to stand strong like Noah. Join with Christian friends and help each other do the right things. By joining together in the fight against sin, you will stand even stronger.

A BRAVE GIRL'S PRAYER

Father, help me love good and hate evil. Please give
me friends who will help me stand strong.

MY BRAVE BEST FRIEND

Don't forget your friend.

PROVERBS 27:10

Her favorite color _____

_____

Her favorite activity _____

_____

Her favorite song _____

_____

Her favorite movie _____

_____

The thing I admire most about her _____

_____

I think she is bravest when _____

_____

She helps me be brave by _____

_____

FOR EXTRA FUN, GIVE THIS SAME LIST TO YOUR
BEST FRIEND AND SEE HOW SHE ANSWERS!

PRICKLY PEOPLE

Stop doing evil and do good. Look
for peace and work for it.

PSALM 34:14

Do you know people who lose their temper quickly? You never know what's going to set them off. And once they're angry, it's hard to settle them down. They can be a little scary to be around! When you find yourself dealing with a prickly person, be brave and remember the porcupine.

Porcupines are large rodents with bushy fur. But their fur is interspersed with sharp, pointy quills—as many as thirty thousand! When a porcupine is relaxed, so are its quills. When it senses danger, though, the porcupine's body tenses, and the quills stand on end. Predators who attempt a bite often leave with a face full of quills! Porcupines grow new quills to replace the ones they lost, so they're always ready for battle.

Now think about your hot-tempered friends. You'll need a little heavenly courage to handle them. Pray and seek God's help for a peaceful way to talk with them. Steer clear of topics you know are upsetting. Over time, they just might learn to trust you and be able to relax in your company, keeping their pointed "quills" flat at their sides.

A BRAVE GIRL'S PRAYER

Lord, give me the courage to be patient with others and
look for ways to keep conversations honoring to You.

SHELL-CENTERED

You are my hiding place. You protect me from my
troubles. You fill me with songs of salvation.

PSALM 32:7

Have you ever seen a turtle tuck its head back inside its shell? Hiding is the turtle's way of protecting itself when it thinks it's in danger. Once it feels safe, the turtle will stretch out its head and begin exploring the world again.

Do you ever feel like that turtle? Do you ever wish you could pull inside your "shell" and hide because you feel shy or scared around others? Sometimes it feels safer to read a book or play on a phone, because we don't know if others will like us or how they'll respond to us. But you don't have to withdraw like a turtle. You have your own protective shell: God. He loves you and thinks you're wonderful just the way you are. So you can walk with confidence into that room filled with people or carry on a conversation with anyone. God's love gives you the courage to come out of your shell and make friends with the people He has placed in your path.

A BRAVE GIRL'S PRAYER

Lord, You are my hiding place. Give me the courage to
talk and connect with others when I am afraid.

AS BRAVE AS A . . .

"Don't let your hearts be troubled. Don't be afraid."

JOHN 14:27

People aren't the only ones who can be afraid—animals get frightened too. And they have their own way of reacting to fear.

TURTLE: She's all about defense. When she feels threatened, she rolls up inside herself, hides away from the world, and doesn't let anyone inside.

SKUNK: When she's frightened, she puts out a stink so big it's sure to scare away any attackers—or even friends!

PORCUPINE: When she's attacked (and sometimes even when she's not!), she bristles up and gets ready to strike.

Do you see yourself in any of these animals? Which one and how?

_____

_____

While these defenses work pretty well for animals, they're not how God wants you to be. What would be a better way to handle your worries and fears? _____

_____

_____

_____

DUCK FEATHERS

Love does not remember wrongs done against it.

1 CORINTHIANS 13:5

Have you heard the saying "Don't worry. Just let it roll off your back"? It means to forget the bad things and focus on the good instead. This saying is inspired by our feathered friends—ducks! Unlike mammals, which have hair, ducks are covered with feathers. Feathers are uniquely made to shelter ducks from wind and rain while also providing the lift they need to fly above predators. To become water repellent, ducks use their bills to spread oil from a gland at the base of their tails to coat their feathers. Then they can float on water, dive underneath it, and even stand in a rainstorm—and the water rolls right off.

In many ways, acting like a duck can help friendships. Because your friends are imperfect, just like you, there will be times when they're selfish instead of serving, or cruel instead of kind. Instead of dumping them, remember the ducks. Let your friends' actions roll off your back and into the forgiveness Jesus offers both them and you. You'll need to be strong—and be sure to ask God to help you. But when you offer kindness and understanding, your friendships will take flight.

A BRAVE GIRL'S PRAYER

Lord, help me not take other people's faults so seriously. Help me forgive them as You forgive me.

ROLL WITH IT

Always be willing to listen and slow to
speak. Do not become angry easily.

JAMES 1:19

Is there a friendship situation that is troubling you now? _____

_____

Are there things you need to let "roll off your back"? _____

_____

Has there been a time when **you** were the difficult friend? _____

_____

Are there things you need to change about what you say and how you
treat your friends? _____

_____

_____

_____

COURAGE TO BE KIND

When you talk, do not say harmful things.
But say what people need—words that
will help others become stronger.

EPHESIANS 4:29

What's the kindest thing anyone has ever done for you? _____

_____

What are the kindest words anyone has ever said to you? _____

_____

What is the kindest thing you've ever done? _____

_____

What are the kindest words you've ever said? _____

_____

Write out your own commitment to be kind here: _____

_____

_____

_____

_____

_____

KINDNESS DOESN'T COST A THING

Be kind and loving to each other.

EPHESIANS 4:32

Allie listened to the speaker from the homeless shelter and felt sad. Not only did she feel terrible about the children at the shelter, but she didn't think she could help them—or anyone. *Lord,* she prayed, *I want to help, but I'm just a kid. I have an allowance, but it's not enough to really help.* Allie looked back at the speaker, only half listening, until something the lady said caught her attention: "Kindness doesn't cost a thing—except maybe a little courage."

That's it! Allie thought. *I may not have lots of money, but I can always be kind! And God will help me have courage!* She tugged a piece of paper out of her notebook and began writing down ideas.

- Invite that new girl to come to the youth group dinner.

- Smile at the cafeteria workers at school.

- Help my little brother tie his shoes.

- Thank my mom for fixing us dinner, and help her clean up.

- Give my dad a hug when he gets home from work.

Maybe you'd like to try some of Allie's ideas. What acts of kindness can you add to her list? _____

_____

_____

_____

— A BRAVE GIRL'S PRAYER —

Lord, I know there's lots of things I can't do yet. But
help me remember that I can always be kind.

BRAVE FACE

Be strong and brave. Don't be afraid of them.
Don't be frightened. The Lord your God will go
with you. He will not leave you or forget you.

DEUTERONOMY 31:6

Mom, I don't want to go in there!" Hayley moaned.

"I'm sure it will be fun," her mom said.

"But I don't know any of those kids," Hayley argued. "They already have their friends. I'm just going to be left out."

"Well, you don't really have a choice. Your dad and I are going to our Sunday school class. I'll come back to get you in an hour."

Hayley went in but took a seat off by herself and stared at the floor.

Have you ever had to be the new person in a group? Change can be difficult, and walking into a place with new faces can be really scary. But you are not alone! God, your Best Friend, is with you wherever you go. And He has a way of connecting His kids with the friends they need. Be brave and trust that God isn't going to abandon you. Instead, He has hidden treasures in the people around you that He eagerly wants you to discover. You can be sure He's working something really good in your life as you reach out to new people with His love.

A BRAVE GIRL'S PRAYER

Lord, fill me with bravery as I face the
challenge of making new friends.

THIS IS ME . . . BEING BRAVE!

"Don't be afraid, because I have saved you.
I have called you by name, and you are mine."

ISAIAH 43:1

What is the bravest thing you have ever done? _____

_____

Does remembering that time you were brave help you when you're scared?

_____

When do you most need to be brave? _____

_____

When is it easiest? Hardest? _____

_____

Draw or attach a picture of your brave self!

BUDDY BUILDING

Let each of us please His neighbor for His
good, to help Him be stronger in faith.

ROMANS 15:2

The big game is on the line. Just one more out, and your team wins. The batter hits a pop-up to center field, and your best friend, Teri, is all set for an easy out. But something goes wrong. She drops the ball! Two runners score, and your team loses. Coming off the field, some of your teammates give Teri the cold shoulder. Others say, "What happened to you out there?" and, "Why didn't you just catch the ball?" You hurt for your friend, but if you stick up for Teri, the team might remember that play *you* missed and turn on you too. What do you do?

a. throw down your glove and walk off alone.
b. join the rest of the team in giving her a hard time.
c. throw an arm over her shoulder and say, "Don't worry about it! We all make mistakes sometimes."

If you picked *C*, then you're a brave buddy builder! Sometimes it takes courage to encourage—especially when everyone else is looking for someone to blame. But that's when your friend needs your encouragement most! Ask God to help you be brave enough to build up your buddies.

A BRAVE GIRL'S PRAYER

Jesus, give me the courage to build up my friends,
especially when everyone else is tearing them down.

NOT GIVING UP!

You should be strong. Don't give up.

2 CHRONICLES 15:7

Has there ever been a time when you were the one who missed the winning shot, got the last out, or somehow messed things up for your friends? _____

_____

_____

How did you feel? _____

_____

Was there someone who comforted you? What happened? _____

_____

What was the one thing you wish someone had done or said to help you feel better? _____

_____

_____

_____

WORD TO THE WISE

THere must be no evil talk among you. . . .
These things are not right for you.

EPHESIANS 5:4

SCENARIO

It wasn't a problem when she was homeschooled, but now that Alli was in a public school, curse words seemed to be everywhere. In fact, taking God's name in vain and adding coarse words to every sentence actually seemed like requirements for fitting in with the cool kids.

It's in all the movies and TV shows my friends watch. I guess it's just unavoidable, she decided.

SOLUTION

If bad language is commonplace in your home or, like Alli, you attend a school or play a sport where everyone else says curse words, then you know how easy it is to start talking like that. Does God care about what you say?

Yes! God wants His children to shine like stars in a dark universe. Many people around us don't know God or what is good and true. By choosing our words wisely and honoring God with what we say, we shine with God's purity and love.

A BRAVE GIRL'S PRAYER

Lord, I want all my words to please You. Fill me with
Your love so that it overflows in what I say.

DARE TO SHARE THE SPOTLIGHT

No one should try to do what will help only himself.
He should try to do what is good for others.

1 CORINTHIANS 10:24

Lexie was the star of the basketball team. If she got the ball, she was almost sure to score. Tonight was the last game, and the team was winning by twenty points. Lexie was playing, but the coach had also put in some girls who didn't get to play often. With just a few seconds left, Lexie got the ball and headed for the basket. Then she saw Angie, who'd never scored before. With a smile, she called, "Hey, Angie!" and passed her the ball. The crowd chanted Angie's name. She went in for a layup and scored!

Lexie could have easily kept the ball and scored again. But she dared to do the unexpected and gave Angie a chance to shine. And for Angie, it was a wonderfully special night.

Think of something you can do better than pretty much anyone you know. While it feels good to make every basket, answer every question, or always be first, dare to be different. Share the spotlight—and let others have a chance to shine.

A BRAVE GIRL'S PRAYER

Lord, thank You for blessing me with my talents. Help me dare to be different and use my talents to help others shine.

MY FABULOUS FRIENDS

A friend loves you all the time.

PROVERBS 17:17

Name _____ We're friends because _____

Name _____ We're friends because _____

Name _____ We're friends because _____

The friend I reach out to first with good news is _____

_____

_____

The friend I reach out to first when I'm hurting is _____

_____

_____

The friend I reach out to for advice is

_____

_____

Friends help us to feel better when we're down and they share in our happiness. Attach pictures of your friends here.

WHOM ARE YOU PLEASING?

We must obey God, not men!

ACTS 5:29

Oh, come on, Annie," Becca pleaded. "We really want you to go to the movies with us Saturday."

"I know," Annie said. "And I want to go, but I've already promised to deliver food with my church group to people who need help."

"Can't you do that any Saturday?" Becca asked. "Besides, I really want you to come and sit by me."

"Yeah, I guess." Annie hesitated. But then she thought about the promise she'd made and said, "But I have to keep my word. I'll try to come with you next time."

It can be hard to say no to friends, but sometimes that's what we have to do. Whether it's saying no to something that's wrong, or even saying no to something good that's just at the wrong time, we have to remember that God should be the One we try to please first. When you're torn between choices, ask yourself whom you're really trying to please. Then, be brave and choose the thing that pleases God.

A BRAVE GIRL'S PRAYER

Lord, help me make good choices, and make my heart want to please You more than people.

CHEATING CHEATS THE CHEATER

When a person gets food dishonestly, it
may taste sweet at first. But later he will
feel as if he has a mouth full of gravel.

PROVERBS 20:17

It would be so easy, Marcie thought. *No one would ever even know.*

She'd gone into Mrs. Stewart's classroom after school to ask a question about tomorrow's test. Mrs. Stewart wasn't there, but the test was! And all the answers were filled in. Marcie stared at it.

Copying down those answers would sure make my life easier, Marcie thought. *I really need a good grade on this test or I won't be able to go on that field trip next week. Plus, I wouldn't have to study so hard, and I could hang out with my friends instead.* What should she do?

As Marcie thought about it, she realized that copying the answers would mean she'd miss out on knowing the things she needed to learn. And even if she missed out on the field trip, she'd feel horrible about betraying Mrs. Stewart's trust. *Cheating would only really cheat me,* she thought. Marcie left the classroom, deciding to wait in the hallway—far away from the temptation of that test.

A BRAVE GIRL'S PRAYER

Lord, help me to remember that cheating only cheats me.

OOPS! and UH-OH!

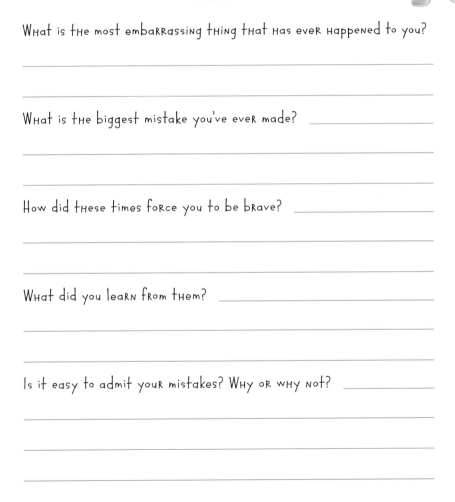

We all make many mistakes.

JAMES 3:2

What is the most embarrassing thing that has ever happened to you?

_____

_____

What is the biggest mistake you've ever made? _____

_____

_____

How did these times force you to be brave? _____

_____

_____

What did you learn from them? _____

_____

_____

Is it easy to admit your mistakes? Why or why not? _____

_____

_____

_____

THE COURAGE TO SAY NO

God says, "Be still and know that I am God."

PSALM 46:10

THE LIE: I NEED TO BE BUSY.

"So, are you going out for the soccer team?" Kate asked.

"N—not sure," Lizzy stammered. "I mean, I haven't decided."

"How about the drama group? Or choir?"

"Probably not."

"Wow. I guess you just like being boring," Kate concluded.

THE TRUTH IS . . .

People today *are* very busy. They're busy with activities and projects. But are people *too* busy? God says that He wants us to be still and know that He is God. When we can barely catch our breath from our activities, we're missing what's most important: time with God.

Why do we stay so busy? Maybe because everyone else seems to be doing it, and they look down on us when we don't. Maybe quiet time makes us nervous. Maybe we feel more important if we're busy. But remember what Jesus told His busy friend, Martha, in Luke 10:38–42: more important than filling our time with activities is filling it with Him. It can take courage to say no to busyness—sometimes it's just easier to say yes. But be brave so that you don't get too busy for Him.

A BRAVE GIRL'S PRAYER

Lord, help me say no to activities I don't need in my life.

MY DaY

Use your time in the best way you can.

COLOSSIANS 4:5

How do you usually spend your hours?

7:00 a.m. _____

8:00 a.m. _____

9:00 a.m. _____

10:00 a.m. _____

11:00 a.m. _____

12:00 p.m. _____

1:00 p.m. _____

2:00 p.m. _____

3:00 p.m. _____

4:00 p.m. _____

5:00 p.m. _____

6:00 p.m. _____

7:00 p.m. _____

8:00 p.m. _____

9:00 p.m. _____

Is there anything you'd like to change about your day? _____

_____

Walking Away

Try hard to live right and to have faith, love,
and peace. Work for these things together
with those . . . who trust in the Lord.

2 TIMOTHY 2:22

Scenario

Emily was thrilled to be invited to the sleepover. She was new in school and trying to make friends. But during the party, the girls decided to watch a scary movie. Emily knew her mom wouldn't approve, so she asked the girls to pick a different one.

"But we all love scary movies!" the host girl responded. "Plus, you don't have to tell your mom."

Solution

Emily could cave to the peer pressure, but what would she get in return? She'd be building friendships with girls who don't value what she does and hurting her relationships with her mom and God. Though it's hard to walk away, Emily would be wise to say, "Okay. Then I'm going upstairs to read. Please let me know when it's over."

We need courage because sometimes we have to walk away from people who aren't ready to follow God. We can be kind and pray for them, but our deep friendships need to be with those who love God too.

A Brave Girl's Prayer

God, give me the courage to walk away from bad friendships.

FINISH THE RACE

I have fought the good fight. I have finished
the race. I have kept the faith.

2 TIMOTHY 4:7

On a scale of 1 to 10, how good are you at finishing a task?

1   2   3   4   5   6   7   8   9   10

We might think, *Well, it depends on the task.* We're more than happy to keep playing that video game until we win. But studying for that test until we really understand the material? Not so much! Persevering—sticking to a task until it's done—is easier when the reward is great.

Jesus understands. The task His Father had given Him wasn't easy at all: leave heaven to suffer on earth while He loved and served people. Then die a horrible death.

That's a tough task! Jesus felt the reward was worth it. He would save all who loved Him, and He would get to be with them forever in heaven. That reward gave Him the courage to finish His task.

Life will not be easy for us either. But God calls us to persevere through every trial, looking to Him for help and trusting in His goodness. When we do, we'll be rewarded with God's peace today and the promise of an eternity in heaven with Him. Knowing that will help give us the courage to finish our race.

A BRAVE GIRL'S PRAYER

Jesus, help me turn to You for strength
whenever I feel like giving up.

THE COURAGE TO KEEP TRYING

Good advice from a friend is sweet.

PROVERBS 27:9

Write about a time a friend gave you the courage to keep trying when you wanted to give up. _____

_____

_____

_____

When did you do the same for a friend? _____

_____

_____

_____

_____

_____

_____

THE BEST LOSER

Everything you say and everything you do
should all be done for Jesus your Lord.

COLOSSIANS 3:17

THE LIE: I NEED TO WIN TO FEEL GOOD ABOUT MYSELF.

"Let's play one more round," Livvy insisted.

"Nooooo," Marlie moaned as she rolled onto her back. "We've played this game, like, three times now!"

"I know, but it isn't fair," Livvy said, growing irritated. "You always get the good cards, so we have to play until I can win."

THE TRUTH IS . . .

While some people are more competitive than others, it's not fun for anybody to lose. And yet someone has to lose in order for someone to win, right? And since it isn't likely—or even fair—that you will always win, then it's just as important to learn to lose well.

Losing well means not having a temper tantrum, accusing others of cheating, or having a bad attitude. It also means being glad for others and grateful for the chance to play at all. That can be hard. But remember: winning doesn't make you a better person. Win or lose, it's your good attitude that makes you the kind of person other people like to play with.

A BRAVE GIRL'S PRAYER

Lord, help me be strong and to win, lose, and
play in a way that shows Your grace.

SWIMMING UPSTREAM

Jesus has the power of God. His power has given
us everything we need to live and to serve God.

2 PETER 1:3

Want to go for a swim? How about a two-thousand-mile-long swim? If you were an Alaskan salmon, that's exactly what you'd do. Salmon hatch from eggs in a freshwater stream in Alaska. As they grow, they travel downstream until they reach the ocean. They spend between one and eight years swimming more than two thousand miles in the Pacific Ocean. Then, amazingly, they find the stream they traveled down years ago and begin the incredibly difficult journey back upstream, jumping up waterfalls and escaping hungry bears along the way. Once they reach their birthplace, the salmon lay eggs, and a new generation takes over the process.

It takes work and determination for salmon to swim upstream. Yet God gifted these creatures with the strength for the journey. You, too, might find that swimming upstream—against the culture—is hard. Wearing the same clothes, listening to the same music, and acting the same way as non-Christians might seem easier, but it wouldn't be better. Be brave! Swim upstream. Because God's way always leads to a greater purpose and new life.

A BRAVE GIRL'S PRAYER

Jesus, please give me strength to swim against the
stream and follow Your way instead of the world's.

FEAR NOT

When I am afraid, I will trust you.

PSALM 56:3

Arachnophobia is the fear of spiders. *Nyctophobia* is fear of the dark. *Glossophobia* is the fear of public speaking. And do you know what *arachibutyrophobia* is? It's the fear of peanut butter sticking to the roof of your mouth! You might laugh, but there's a big, fancy word for every fear—and everybody's afraid of something.

Even the heroes of the Bible were afraid at times. Moses was afraid of Pharaoh, Esther was afraid to go to the king, and all the disciples were afraid when Jesus was arrested. But God was with each and every one of them. He helped Moses face Pharaoh, He helped Esther save her people, and He gave the disciples the courage to come back to Him.

So whether you're afraid of spending the night away from home, standing up to a bully, or even opening the peanut butter jar, God will help you face your fears. It's His promise: "I am with you. Don't be afraid . . . I will make you strong and will help you" (Isaiah 41:10).

A BRAVE GIRL'S PRAYER

God, You are my Defender, my Protector, my Fortress, and my Shield. I will trust You to help me when I'm afraid.

WINNER GIVES ALL

"It is more blessed to give than to receive."

ACTS 20:35

Jesus shows us that one of the best ways to be a friend is to give up your rights to serve others. But living selflessly isn't easy—it takes courage *and* strength to put others before yourself. Take this quiz to test whether you tend to be a taker or a giver.

Your mom just brought home a bag of candy from the store. You:

❏ A. Take some candy for yourself and hide the rest so the others won't find it

❏ B. Go tell all your brothers and sisters so you can all share the fun

It's time for everyone to get in the car, but there are a lot of people to fit in. You:

❏ A. Rush to get into the best seat and make others crawl over you to get situated

❏ B. Volunteer to sit in the back so others won't have to crawl over

You are starting to feel alone and wish you had someone to play with. You:

❏ A. Get angry at your friends for not thinking of you and inviting you over

❏ B. Pick up the phone and ask your friends to come over for a visit

You are listening to music in the car, but your brother wants to hear something else. You:

❑ A. Say, "Too bad. I was listening to this first."

❑ B. Say, "Okay, why don't we take turns listening to music we like?" and turn the station.

SURVEY SAYS

GIVER: If you answered *B* to these questions, you are growing a servant's heart like Jesus.

TAKER: If you answered *A* to any of the above, ask yourself whom it is you are serving in that scenario. Then ask God to give you a servant's heart like His Son's.

A SECOND CHANCE

"If you forgive others for the things they do wrong, then your Father in heaven will also forgive you for the things you do wrong."

MATTHEW 6:14

As soon as the rooster crowed, Peter knew he'd made a horrible choice. Instead of standing strong and supporting Jesus after the soldiers arrested Him, Peter acted as if he didn't know Jesus. Peter knew he'd been a terrible friend and didn't deserve a second chance (Mark 14:66–72).

But that's not how Jesus saw it. After Jesus rose again, He appeared to Peter and let him know that all was forgiven. Jesus wanted Peter to stay His friend (John 21:15–19).

Have you ever hurt your friends' feelings by doing something mean? Or have they done something wrong to you? Jesus reminds us how important it is to forgive others when they hurt us. If you have a friendship that needs mending, don't wait another minute. Be brave. Call your friend, and work out the problem. Have the courage to admit if you've done anything wrong. Then ask for forgiveness or forgive your friend. Take the second chance, and put the past behind you both.

A BRAVE GIRL'S PRAYER

Father, thank You for forgiving all my sins. Please give me the courage and strength to forgive others too.

YOU BEING YOU

Do not love the world or the things in the world.

1 JOHN 2:15

Sarah stared at herself in the dressing room mirror, tugging at the skirt, and twisting it this way and that. *It's just so short*, she thought.

"Don't you love it?" Becca asked.

"Well . . ." Sarah stalled. "I'm not sure my mom would approve. And I'm not sure it's for me."

"Oh, come on," Becca nagged. "*Everybody* wears them now. Don't you want to be like everybody else?"

Sarah thought for a second, bravely shook her head, and reached for her jeans. "Nope," she said with a smile. "I want to be me."

Did you ever play dress-up when you were younger, pretending to be someone else? A movie star, a teacher, a doctor, or a princess? Pretending to be someone else is a great way to play, but it's a lousy way to live. God created you in an amazing way and blessed you in your uniqueness. Don't be afraid to be the wonderful person God made you to be!

A BRAVE GIRL'S PRAYER

Lord, I keep hearing about all the things I should do and say and wear so I'll fit in. Help me not to be afraid to be me.

ALL DRESSED UP!

He has covered me with a coat of goodness. . . .
I am like a bride dressed in jewels.

ISAIAH 61:10

My favorite outfit is _____

_____

I love this outfit because _____

_____

_____

I feel stronger and braver when I wear _____ because

_____

Attach or draw a picture of you in your favorite outfit.

A Tempting Idea

When you are tempted, God will also give
you a way to escape that temptation.

1 CORINTHIANS 10:13

Look at the list of temptations below. Which ones do you find hardest to fight?

- keeping the whole bag of candy for yourself instead of sharing

- telling that juicy bit of gossip about the new girl in school

- writing the answers to the test on your hand

- yelling at siblings when they get on your nerves

Making the right choice can feel impossible when everything inside us wants to cave in to temptation. We're only human, right? Who could expect us to do the right thing in that situation?

Jesus could, that's who! But He isn't standing around, waiting for you to mess up. He understands exactly how you feel because when He was on earth, He was tempted too. But Jesus was able to stand strong against every temptation—and He can help you do the same.

Whenever you turn to Jesus for help in a tempting situation, you're trusting in His secret source of strength: the goodness and power of God.

A Brave Girl's Prayer

Jesus, thank You for understanding my
weakness. Help me be strong in You.

COURAGE TO SPEAK THE TRUTH

We will speak the truth with love. We will grow up
in every way to be like Christ, who is the head.

EPHESIANS 4:15

We know it's not right to lie. But telling the truth isn't always easy, especially when the truth might hurt someone. You know what's even harder? Learning to tell the truth with God's love. Check out these scenarios, and see how you rank at truth-telling God's way: with courage, love, and a humble heart.

Your friend's zipper is down. You:

- ☐ A. pretend nothing's wrong.
- ☐ B. start laughing uncontrollably and pointing.
- ☐ C. whisper the embarrassing fact in her ear.

The teacher is writing on the board, and you notice that she misspelled a word. You:

- ☐ A. blurt out to the class that she can't spell.
- ☐ B. laugh with your friends about her mistake.
- ☐ C. raise your hand and go up to ask her to tell her about the error.

Your best friend forgot your birthday. You:

- ❑ A. give her the silent treatment for a whole week.
- ❑ B. tell all your other friends how awful she is.
- ❑ C. wait until she's alone and admit that her forgetting really hurt your feelings.

You met a new girl at the park who doesn't think Jesus is real. You:

- ❑ A. get really angry and tell her she's stupid for not believing in Jesus.
- ❑ B. get scared of her and stop playing with her altogether.
- ❑ C. calmly and lovingly explain why you believe that Jesus is God's Son and continue to treat her with kindness and respect.

If you answered *C* for all of the above, then congratulations! You have learned the secret to sharing the truth with God's love courageously. If you chose some other options, think of why those actions aren't very love-filled and can hurt others. Then pray and ask God to help you always tell the truth in love, just like how God speaks to you in His Word.

WHAT REALLY MATTERS

To God every person is the same. God accepts anyone who worships Him and does what is right. It is not important what country a person comes from.

ACTS 10:34–35

Hope dropped her backpack on the bus seat and huffed out a big sigh.

"What's wrong?" her friend asked.

"I heard some kids making fun of my little brothers," Hope said, "because they still have a little bit of a Ukrainian accent. Those kids even said some mean stuff about their being adopted. Can you believe that?"

Hope's friend shook her head sadly.

It's easy to look at others and see all the things that make them different from us. They don't look the same, sound the same, or dress the same. And some people use those differences as a reason not to like people, to make fun of them, or to bully them.

It takes a brave person to look for all the ways we're the same and to look for reasons to reach out and connect. All our differences don't matter one bit to God. Every single person is His beloved creation, and we all matter to Him.

A BRAVE GIRL'S PRAYER

God, help me to see each and every person as someone You love.

COUNT ON IT!

God does not change.

JAMES 1:17

Does it ever seem like the whole world is changing? Friendships are changing. Some people move away, and others move in. We change schools, and our parents change jobs. Even our own bodies are changing. Some days it's hard to know what to expect—or whom we can count on!

But one thing is for certain: we can always count on God. He never changes—not ever! The promises He made thousands and thousands of years ago He still keeps today, like when He told Joshua that He would never leave him (Joshua 1:5), or when He promised in Matthew that He would take care of everything we need (6:25–34), or when He promised to save all of us who choose to follow Jesus. Those promises weren't just for the people of the Bible. They're for us too.

It takes a lot of courage to live in a world that's constantly changing. One thing that will help you be brave is knowing this fabulous fact: God always keeps His promises. You can count on it!

A BRAVE GIRL'S PRAYER

God, help me to see each and every person as someone You love.

THE PEOPLE-PLEASER PIT

If I wanted to please men, I would
not be a servant of Christ.

GALATIANS 1:10

THE LIE: I NEED EVERYONE TO LIKE ME.

Erika's stomach hurt because of stress. Some other girls wanted her to join them on the soccer team. But God had gifted her better at dance. *If I choose dance instead of soccer, all those girls are going to get mad,* Erika reasoned. *And I don't want to deal with that all year.*

The next day Erika decided to go out for the soccer team. "It's just easier that way," she said.

THE TRUTH IS . . .

We really only need to please one person, and you won't find Him in your yearbook. And the great news is that God is already pleased with you.

God hasn't given you the impossible task of making everyone like you. Instead, He *has* asked you to follow Him and do what He's called you to do. That will take courage sometimes. But when you seek to please God instead of people, your joy and strength in God will grow, no matter what others may do or say.

A BRAVE GIRL'S PRAYER

Lord, I want to please You with all I say and do. Help
me keep my focus on You and not my friends.

FROM A DISTANCE

Do not be fooled: "Bad friends will ruin good habits."

1 CORINTHIANS 15:33

Lexie was struggling. She tried to be friends with everyone, so when a couple of girls from her class invited her to go swimming, she agreed. But while she was with them, the girls started gossiping, and said a lot of things that were both cruel and untrue. *It's like they enjoy hurting people,* Lexie thought. Lexie called her mom to pick her up early. As she left, the girls invited her to come again, but Lexie thought to herself, *I'm not sure that's a good idea.*

Lexie's right. God wants us to try to be friends with everyone, but some people actually seem to enjoy doing wrong. We should still forgive them because that's what God asks. And we should pray for them, but we should also have the courage to stay away—even if they're part of that group we really want to fit in with. Because if we get too close, their bad habits could easily start to ruin our good ones. It happened to Samson with Delilah (Judges 16), and it happened to King Solomon with his wives (1 Kings 11).

So, yes, be kind to everyone and pray for those who aren't kind—but have the courage to do it from a distance.

A BRAVE GIRL'S PRAYER

God, help me to choose friends who will encourage me to follow You.

"BRAVE" ANOTHER WAY

God will strengthen you with His own great power.
And you will not give up when troubles come.

COLOSSIANS 1:11

Synonyms are different words that mean the same—or almost the same thing. Search the puzzle to find all these different words for *brave*. Then you can use a concordance or a Bible search engine to look up different verses about being brave.

BRAVE

COURAGEOUS

STRONG

MIGHTY

VALIANT

BOLD

DARING

HEROIC

```
S   R   U   F   V   G   W   Q   X   E   Y   Y
T   M   L   F   M   A   V   M   D   V   B   O
R   J   H   J   D   Q   L   L   O   A   G   W
O   F   G   L   O   D   Z   I   E   R   F   X
N   R   O   J   X   M   O   A   A   B   R   M
G   B   Q   P   I   V   G   Q   U   N   V   Y
T   G   C   G   I   F   F   G   H   K   T   J
X   J   H   I   L   S   R   U   B   J   J   C
H   T   Q   B   O   U   B   Y   N   M   G   A
Y   S   C   O   U   R   A   G   E   O   U   S
G   N   I   R   A   D   E   Z   V   E   R   Z
J   B   P   S   T   L   E   H   A   A   M   C
```

IMPOSSIBLE POSSIBLE

"For people this is impossible. But for
God all things are possible."

MARK 10:27

You've got to be kidding me! Alana thought, slamming her books down on the desk. *How am I supposed to work with Tiffany? She's been so mean to me! God,* she silently prayed, *I know I'm supposed to love my enemies, but I just don't think I can do it!*

Tiffany had been making fun of Alana all year long— her clothes, her hair, even the way she talked. And now they were assigned to work together on a project. That's a tough assignment! On her own, Alana couldn't begin to figure out a way to be kind to Tiffany, much less work together and help her.

Fortunately, Alana isn't on her own—and neither are we. God is always with us, giving us the courage and strength to do what's right. With His help, those things that seem impossible to us become possible, things like being kind to those who've hurt us and forgiving our enemies. When we're faced with an impossible task, let's reach out to God and ask for His courage, strength, and wisdom. He makes the impossible possible!

A BRAVE GIRL'S PRAYER

God, thank You for being strong when I'm
not. Help me remember that You're always
there to help me do the right thing.

Starting Over

Rahab was supposed to be one of Israel's enemies. Living in Jericho, she had probably done many of the evil deeds that had made God angry at the nation. But when she heard about God, she wanted to change sides.

So when Israel sent spies into Jericho, she hid them in her home. Then she helped them escape in exchange for her family's safety when Israel attacked the city. Because Rahab chose to side with God, only she and her family survived when God gave the city to the Israelites. Best of all, Rahab was accepted into the Hebrew family of God (Joshua 2; 6:22–25).

Sometimes we can find ourselves in a situation like Rahab's. We realize we've been living a life that displeases God. But Rahab's story gives us great hope! God always welcomes us when we turn to Him for help. So confess your bad choices to God, and ask Him to shape you into the person He wants you to be. Starting over isn't always easy—and you'll need to be brave—but God will help you through it!

A BRAVE GIRL'S PRAYER

Father, please forgive my sin of _____.
Save me, and make me Your own.

A BRAVE LADY

The Lord has blessed you and is with you.

LUKE 1:28

If you quickly read through Matthew 1, it might seem like just another boring list of names. But take a closer look: there are some ladies—brave ladies—hidden in all those names. One of those ladies was Mary, the mother of Jesus. Read about Mary in Luke 1–2 and Matthew 1.

Imagine yourself in Mary's shoes. What might she have been thinking and feeling:

When the angel told her the news? _____

When she visited Elizabeth? _____

When she told Joseph the news? _____

When she traveled to Bethlehem? _____

When the innkeeper said there was no room for them? _____

When she first held Jesus in her arms? _____

When the shepherds appeared? _____

What do you think made Mary so brave? _____

"DO YOU LOVE ME?"

[Peter] answered, "Yes, Lord, you
know that I love you."
Jesus said, "Take care of my sheep."

JOHN 21:16

Peter had blown it in the worst way imaginable. After spending years with Jesus, he had abandoned his Lord when the soldiers arrested Jesus. He had run away in fear and told everyone who asked that he didn't even know Jesus!

After Jesus was crucified and rose again, He appeared to Peter. But Jesus didn't say, "I told you so," or, "You're a terrible friend." Instead, He asked Peter, "Do you love Me?"

His question reached deep into Peter's heart. Peter thought about it and said, "Yes, I love You."

"Then feed My sheep," answered Jesus. Jesus was telling Peter that he was forgiven, and if he loved Him, then he needed to take care of the people who loved Jesus.

Jesus asks you the same question. "Do you love Me, Brave Girl?" Think about it and be completely honest. If the answer is yes, then you're completely forgiven too. Let that beautiful knowledge give you the courage to join Jesus in bringing lost sheep to the Great Shepherd.

A BRAVE GIRL'S PRAYER

I want to show that I truly love You, Lord,
by bravely obeying and following You.

HOW DO YOU LOVE JESUS?

"Love the Lord your God. Love Him with
all your heart, all your soul, all your
mind, and all your strength."

MARK 12:30

Write a letter to Jesus, telling Him how and why you love Him.

_____

_____

_____

_____

_____

_____

_____

_____

_____

_____

NOT-SO-BRAVE SOMETIMES

You want me to be completely
truthful. So teach me wisdom.

PSALM 51:6

Job wasn't happy. In just a short time, God had allowed Satan to send a horrible storm that destroyed Job's home and killed all his children. Then his crops were destroyed, and his health fell to pieces. Even Job's wife encouraged him to curse God and die.

Job didn't curse God, but he did want to know why these things had happened. Without holding back, Job cried out to God, asking for understanding and relief.

And guess what? Even though God didn't answer his question, He talked to Job and comforted him. God wasn't afraid of Job's questions. With power, holiness, and love, God helped Job to grow in his trust and love of Him. (Read the whole story in the book of Job.)

Do you have questions or frustrations about the way God runs His world? Have you had sad things happen that you just don't understand? It's okay to feel not-so-brave sometimes, even a bit worried and scared. Don't bother hiding your feelings. Bring them to God. Talk to Him as Job did. You may not get all the answers you're looking for, but God will give you peace and comfort you with His love.

A BRAVE GIRL'S PRAYER

God, thanks for handling my tough questions and
loving me when I'm hurt and confused.

TOTAL CONNECTION

At that time Jesus went off to a mountain to
pray. He stayed there all night, praying to God.

LUKE 6:12

When should you pray? Which of these times are most worthy of prayer?

- You are nervous about a test at school.

- You have just woken up in the morning.

- Your parent is sick.

- You won the spelling bee.

- You are scared to share your faith.

- You yelled at your mom.

These are all great times to pray! God wants us to pray all the time—whether we're sad, scared, happy, unsure, excited, or mad. Through prayer, we invite God into every part of our lives, sharing everything with Him and looking for Him to enjoy it with us or help us through it. Prayer draws us closer to God.

It takes courage not only to invite God into our lives, but also to trust Him to answer our prayers. When we do that, we show that we trust and love God the same way Jesus did when He was on earth. Jesus prayed all the time. And if we want to walk in Jesus' footsteps, we need to depend on God the same way—through prayer.

A BRAVE GIRL'S PRAYER

Lord, thank You for inviting me to be close
to You through the gift of prayer.

BIGGER THAN BIG

David said to Him, "You come to me using a sword,
a large spear and a small spear. But I come to
you in the name of the Lord of Heaven's armies."

1 SAMUEL 17:45

Goliath was bigger than big, huger than huge, the soldier of all soldiers. And David was definitely . . . *not*.

In fact, when David faced Goliath, he wasn't a soldier at all. David was only a shepherd boy. He was just out checking on his brothers. He wasn't even supposed to fight. But David saw that Goliath was a problem, and he also saw that no one else was willing to fix it. So David did what needed to be done. He went out to fight Goliath. But the thing is, he didn't go on his own.

David went in *the name of the Lord*.

He didn't have a shield or a spear, but he had God. And he knew that would be more than enough.

When we face a big problem—a Goliath of a problem—we don't have to be afraid. We just need to remember who our God is. He's bigger than any problem, and God always fights for us.

A BRAVE GIRL'S PRAYER

When my problems seem so big, Lord, help me
remember that You are always bigger.

peace Talks

"Those who work to bring peace are happy."

MATTHEW 5:9

So often, when we think about being brave, we think about being willing to fight for what is right. But just as often, being brave is about making peace. In fact, it can require just as much—and sometimes more!—courage than being ready to fight. But have you ever wondered why God wants His people to be keepers of His peace?

Think about it this way: people are always divided in fights, right? But God created us to be one big, happy family, serving Him and loving each other. What keeps that from happening? Sin! It separates us from each other and God. It was such a big problem that God sent Jesus to die (and rise again) so that we could have peace. One day, when His children are in heaven, we'll all love Him and each other in perfect unity.

But for now, God wants each of us to play our role in keeping peace here on earth. It helps others see God's plan and want to be with Him too, so it's a really important job for us. So when we see a fight or disagreement about to begin, let's pray, ask God for wisdom, and seek peace.

A BRAVE GIRL'S PRAYER

Jesus, please give me Your peace. Help me
keep it daily in my life with others.

"PEACE-ING" IT ALL TOGETHER

Try to live in peace with all people.

HEBREWS 12:14

Think about some of the following situations, and decide how you would start the peace process.

Your friends have stopped speaking to each other because they're mad. You:

_____

_____

Your family is arguing because they can't agree on a restaurant. You:

_____

_____

Your sister keeps whispering to you and giggling during the sermon at church. You: _____

_____

_____

You got angry with your brother and said some pretty mean things during the fight. You: _____

_____

_____

SPEAK UP

Speak up for those who cannot speak for themselves.

PROVERBS 31:8

Onesimus was in a bit of trouble. He had been a slave, but he ran away. Then Onesimus met Paul, who told him about Jesus. Onesimus repented of his sins and turned to Jesus as his Savior.

Now it was time for Onesimus to go back to his master's family. Paul wanted him to return not only to mend the bad relationships, but also to share all the good things God had taught him through Paul. But Paul didn't send Onesimus back empty-handed. He gave him a letter—what is now the book of Philemon—asking the family to receive Onesimus not as a slave, but as a brother in Christ! Since the family members were also believers, Paul trusted they would welcome Onesimus back as a beloved child of God's family.

Paul knew that going back would be difficult for Onesimus. So he helped by speaking up for him. Do you speak up for your friends? Oftentimes, you'll have to be brave to do it. But whether it's asking a parent or teacher for help, or remembering to pray for them daily, good friends speak up for one another and are loyal to the end.

A BRAVE GIRL'S PRAYER

Lord, help me remember to pray for my friends and to stick up for them when they need help.

STICKING UP and STICKING TOGETHER

Defend the rights of the poor and suffering.

PSALM 82:3

Have you ever had someone stick up for you? What happened?

_____

_____

How did it feel to know that someone was on your side? _____

_____

_____

Are there people you can stick up for? Who? _____

_____

_____

God is always on your side. What does knowing that mean to you?

_____

_____

LIFE OR DEATH

"The words I told you are spirit,
and so they give life."

JOHN 6:63

Have you ever noticed how a mean comment from a friend can ruin your whole day? On the other hand, a simple hug or encouraging word can make your spirit sing. Don't worry. We are all that way! God created us to respond to the power of words. It's one of the reasons God gave the Bible to us. Through His words, we learn how to live life and find Jesus. God's words are powerful enough to change lives.

But your words are powerful too. And it takes courage and self-control to use them in the right way. Each time you open your mouth, you can choose to speak words that will help others know how valuable they are or how worthless you think they are. You can speak words of life to them or words of death. As very loved children of God, we no longer have any need to hurt others with our words. Instead, God has given us the mission to build up others, encouraging them in their faith and lives. Sometimes it can be very difficult, especially if that person or family member says mean things to you. It's natural to want to fight back. But it isn't God's way. God is love—so have the courage to let your words show it!

A BRAVE GIRL'S PRAYER

Jesus, fill my mouth with loving words that
come from Your heart and help others.

THAT UNLOVED FEELING

The Lord's love never ends.
LAMENTATIONS 3:22

Leah probably always knew her younger sister was prettier than she was. When Jacob first came to their land, it was Rachel who caught his attention and won his love. But after Jacob worked for seven years to marry Rachel, Leah and Rachel's father tricked Jacob into marrying Leah instead. This made Jacob upset, of course, so he worked another seven years to marry Rachel. All her life, Leah probably knew she wasn't the prettiest or the most wanted in the group. Yet God loved her. He chose her to be the mother of many sons who grew to become the first leaders of Israel. He had great plans for Leah that were far more important than how she looked on the outside. (Read about Leah in Genesis 29–30).

Maybe you can relate to Leah. Sometimes kids can be mean and leave you out of the group or make you feel unimportant. And if you believe other people look better than you do, you can feel bad about yourself. But Leah's story lets you know that no matter what, you are a treasure in God's eyes. When others are unloving and unkind, be brave and remember that God has promised you a future full of hope and His never-ending love.

A BRAVE GIRL'S PRAYER

Father, give me courage when others are unkind.
And help me remember that I am special—
simply because I was made by You.

BIRDS OF A FEATHER

"Your Heavenly Father feeds the birds. And you know that you are worth much more than the birds. You cannot add any time to your life by worrying about it."

MATTHEW 6:26–27

Everything seemed to be spinning out of control. Anna's father had gotten a great new job, but now they were moving. For Anna that meant leaving behind everything she knew and starting over in a new home, a new school, and even a new church. *What if I don't fit in?* she worried. *What if no one likes me?*

Changes—even good changes—can be hard. Jesus understands that. After all, He moved from heaven to earth. Talk about a big change! When you're facing changes, it's easy to let worries and what-ifs take over your thoughts. If that happens, stop and remember the birds. God knows each and every feather on each and every bird. He watches over them and cares for them. And you're much more important than birds to God. So just think of how much more God will care for you—and let His love make you brave!

A BRAVE GIRL'S PRAYER

Lord, when everything is changing, help me remember that You're watching over me—and that's one thing that will never change!

BRAVE BELIEVING

You have been saved by grace because you believe.
You did not save yourselves. It was a gift from God.

EPHESIANS 2:8

A dad from Israel came to Jesus and asked Him to heal his son (Mark 9:14–27). The boy had been tormented by an evil spirit since he was a very young child. What's worse, Jesus' disciples seemed unable to cast it out of the boy. So when the man came to Jesus, he wasn't totally sure Jesus could help either. "If you can help him, please do," the man pleaded to Jesus.

"If you can?" Jesus questioned his doubt. "Everything is possible for one who believes."

So there it was: hope. All the dad had to do was believe. The problem was that the man knew in his heart he still had doubts. "Lord, I do believe. Help me to believe more!" he cried out. He knew he needed help in every way, even with having faith. So Jesus answered both requests, and the boy was healed.

Believing requires bravery—especially when the problem seems impossible to fix. Fortunately, Jesus is there to help you with both your believing and your bravery. Just ask Him for help—He would love to answer you.

A BRAVE GIRL'S PRAYER

Jesus, please help me to be brave enough to believe in You.

BRAVE ENOUGH TO REST

"Come with me. We will go to a quiet place to
be alone. There we will get some rest."

MARK 6:31

Katie stared at the family calendar on the refrigerator.
Soccer practice every afternoon, youth group
meeting Wednesday, piano practice Thursday, and a
family dinner at Grandma's Friday—plus homework
and chores. It was going to be a busy week. *These are
all great things,* Katie thought, *but I'm already feeling tired,
and it's only Tuesday!*

Even as kids, our schedules can get very busy. Jesus understands
because His schedule was often *very* busy with teaching, healing, and
traveling. Sometimes He and His disciples didn't even have time to eat!
But Jesus also knew the importance of rest. He'd often slip away from
everyone and everything simply to talk to His Father and rest.

If rest was important for Jesus, how much more important is it for
you? It might take some courage to say no to some things, but try to find
time every day—even just a minute or two—to slip away, talk to God, and
rest. Go to your room, go outside, or simply close your eyes right where
you are. Because Brave Girls take time to rest in God.

A BRAVE GIRL'S PRAYER

Lord, some days are so busy that I forget to talk
to You. But I'm so glad You never forget me.

ON THE ROUGH DAYS

The Lord is close to the brokenhearted.

PSALM 34:18

It had been a really rough day. Gracie dropped her backpack on the floor and slumped down on her bed. She'd bombed the test and, in her worry, had snapped at a friend. Now she realized that she'd forgotten to put away her laundry, and her mom was sure to be upset. As tears of frustration filled her eyes, she looked up and simply prayed, *God?*

We all have days when nothing seems to go right. But no matter the trouble, if it's our own fault or someone else's, God is there to listen and to help. You don't even have to know the words to say. Just open up and let all those worries, frustrations, and hurt feelings pour out to Him. Then turn to His Word, and let Him pour His answers into you with promises like, "I will never leave you" (Hebrews 13:5), "The Lord is close to the brokenhearted" (Psalm 34:18), and, "Nothing can separate us from the love God has for us" (Romans 8:38).

Turn to God . . . because He understands that sometimes even Brave Girls have bad days.

A BRAVE GIRL'S PRAYER

God, I'm so grateful that You always listen and understand. I know You'll help me.

FIRST THINGS FIRST

Then the king said to me, "What do you want?"
First I prayed to the God of heaven.

NEHEMIAH 2:4

When you're faced with a difficult choice or a tough situation, what do you do first?

Nehemiah, a Jew, was in a tough situation. He'd been taken from his home in Jerusalem and was now a servant to the king of Persia. But he had heard that Jerusalem was in terrible trouble. Its walls were falling down, and enemies were threatening to attack. He wanted to go home to help. But first he had to get the king's permission. He was so nervous.

Later, when Nehemiah was serving at the king's table, the king could tell something was wrong. "Why does your face look sad?" the king asked. "What do you want?" But before Nehemiah answered, he prayed to God. And as it turned out, Nehemiah convinced the king to help!

When you're not sure what to say or what to do, follow Nehemiah's example and pray first. God promises that if you ask Him for wisdom, He will give it to you. In fact, the Bible says He enjoys giving wisdom to His people (James 1:5). When you're not sure what to do or say, talk to God—first!

A BRAVE GIRL'S PRAYER

Lord, help me remember to turn to You
first when I have troubles.

THE HARDEST THING . . .

The Lord gives . . . power to those who are weak.

ISAIAH 40:29

What is the hardest thing you've ever had to do? _____

_____

_____

How did you have to be brave to do it? _____

_____

_____

What or who helped you to be brave? _____

_____

_____

SUMMER STORMS

You are my hiding place and my
shield. I trust your word.

PSALM 119:114

*C*rash! You are jolted awake by thunder. *Flash!* Lightning illuminates the sky outside your window. And then you hear the sound of rain, slow at first, but then pouring all around. Grateful for the shelter of your house, you snuggle deeper under the covers, waiting for the storm to be over.

Storms can be scary sometimes, can't they? Storms can make us feel powerless and vulnerable, even though we know the rain is good for the earth.

But storms are good for reminding us of God's tremendous power! As big as storms get and as strong as the lightning seems, God is even bigger and stronger. He not only made the world that houses those storms, He created the universe, which holds everything else! Our God is really, really big and powerful. And He's the perfect shelter from the storms—not just rainstorms, but storms of life, such as sickness, sadness, or separation. When we're afraid and need a little help to be brave, let's go to God—in prayer, in His Word, or simply sitting with Him. He'll keep us safe in His care!

A BRAVE GIRL'S PRAYER

Father, thank You for watching over me and keeping me safe.

STRONGER THAN ANY STORM

Even the wind and the waves obey Him!

MARK 4:41

What's the biggest storm you've ever seen? _____

_____

_____

Were you frightened? _____

_____

Besides the weather, what other kinds of storms have you faced in your life? _____

_____

_____

_____

Who and what helped calm your storms? _____

_____

_____

_____

TRUTH TELLING

"You must not tell lies."

EXODUS 23:1

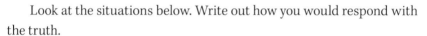

We know we should tell the truth and lying is bad. But have we ever wondered why? Jesus says that when we tell a lie, we are acting like we belong to Satan instead of God. But when we speak the truth, we're talking God's language—and His words are powerful!

Look at the situations below. Write out how you would respond with the truth.

- You accidentally broke your mom's necklace. You could hide it back in her jewelry drawer, but instead you:

- The kids at church were complaining that church was dumb. You want them to like you, but you don't agree with them. So you say:

- Your friend hurt your feelings when she ignored you at lunch. You could pretend everything was okay, but instead you bravely and lovingly tell her:

It isn't always easy to tell the truth, and sometimes you have to be really brave. But God will always help you do what's right when you ask Him.

A BRAVE GIRL'S PRAYER

Lord, please keep me from telling lies, even in what seems to be small ways. Give me the courage always to tell the truth.

LOUSY LIES

Truth will last forever. But lies last only a moment.

PROVERBS 12:19

Have you ever given in to the temptation to lie? _____

_____

_____

What happened? Did you get caught? _____

_____

_____

How did lying make you feel? _____

_____

_____

If you could relive that moment, would you tell the truth instead?

_____

_____

Have you ever been lied to by a friend? How did you feel when you

found out? _____

_____

_____

LADY IN WAITING

Be strong and brave and wait for the Lord's help.

PSALM 27:14

Sarah handled moving from home like a champ. She even trusted God to take care of her when her husband, Abraham, gave her some risky instructions. But waiting for a baby? That was tough. Years passed, and she still didn't have a baby. So she panicked and had her maidservant, Hagar, bear a child for her. But that wasn't God's answer.

While Sarah waited, she grew old—like gray-hair-and-rocking-chair old. But one day God sent a messenger to tell her she would have a baby! Her wrinkled face smiled, and then she laughed. *How could a woman my age have a baby?* she thought. But in less than a year, Sarah had baby Isaac (Genesis 21:1–7).

Sarah's story shows the beauty of waiting on God. Worrying or trying to make things happen the way we want only frustrates us and keeps us from watching God work miracles. When we wait patiently for God to meet our needs, we learn to trust that He will keep His promises. Yes, we'll need to be brave—but the rewards are heavenly!

A BRAVE GIRL'S PRAYER

Lord, help me to be patient and wait for You to lead me.

DEFINING BEAUTY

You are beautiful! Oh, you are beautiful!

SONG OF SOLOMON 1:15

What is beauty? It depends on where you live. In the United States, the media prize slender girls with flawless skin, big eyes, and long hair. But people in Mauritania and Nigeria believe the bigger the woman, the more beautiful she is! If you lived in the Pa Dong tribe near Thailand, you'd want a long neck—a look achieved by adding metal rings around your neck each year, starting at age six. And if you lived with the Maori in New Zealand, you'd value tattooed blue lips.

The truth is, our ideas about beauty come from what other people around us say—and those ideas change all the time. Trying to meet everybody's expectations is not only exhausting, it's silly! We were made to show our Creator's creativity and love through our different looks, personalities, and styles as we live lives all about loving others. The Bible says to stop comparing ourselves to other people, stop trying to be like them or better than them. Instead, God says to be bold, brave, and be-you-tiful!

A BRAVE GIRL'S PRAYER

Father, You have told me in so many ways that I am beautiful to You. Please help me to listen only to You!

WORTH SEARCH

You belong to the Lord your God. He has chosen
you from all the people on earth to be His very own.

DEUTERONOMY 14:2

We all want to know what we're worth, and we hope it's enough to please God. But we don't have to hope. We can know that we are priceless in God's eyes because of what He says in His Word. Read these passages, and then find these words in the word search—they describe who you are in Jesus. Knowing *who* you are will help you feel a little more brave.

NEW (Ephesians 2:10)

WITNESS (Acts 1:8)

CHOSEN (Ephesians 1:4)

LOVED (2 Thessalonians 2:17)

SOLDIER (2 Timothy 2:3)

FORGIVEN (1 John 1:9)

FRIEND (James 2:23)

TEMPLE (1 Corinthians 3:16)

CHILD (John 1:12)

T	H	L	C	N	L	G	F	R	C
F	E	C	G	O	V	O	P	M	H
N	W	M	V	C	R	R	E	K	I
F	K	E	P	G	B	N	R	R	L
X	D	B	I	L	E	F	J	E	D
P	R	V	S	S	E	N	T	I	W
W	E	N	O	J	A	J	N	D	X
N	M	H	F	Q	T	P	B	L	S
W	C	F	R	I	E	N	D	O	K
M	H	T	E	B	C	H	F	S	P

Hang in There!

I will still be glad in the Lord. I will rejoice in God
my Savior. The Lord God gives me my strength.

HABAKKUK 3:18–19

Nothing going right?
Have you had days when it seemed there
was a black cloud hanging over your head? Your
mom's car wouldn't start, and you were late to
school. When you got there, you found out you'd
left your homework on the kitchen table. When
you got home, your sister had eaten the last of the
cookies.

Habakkuk 3:18–19 is part of a song of praise during the storms of life.
The author was struggling just to make it through, but he still praised
God and had hope. It's easy to have hope when things are going smoothly,
but to have hope when things are bad requires a bold and brave faith. So
gather up your courage and stand tall! Take a deep breath, say a prayer,
keep doing right, and trust God to make something good out of the
wrong. And remember, soon the sun will set on this day, and God will
give you another chance to start fresh in the morning.

A Brave Girl's Prayer

Lord, help me to be brave on those days when
it seems like nothing is going right. I know that
with You by my side, everything will be okay.

ON THE HUNT

Be careful! The devil is your enemy. And he goes
around like a roaring lion looking for someone to eat.

1 PETER 5:8

Who's the king of the savanna? The lion, of course. Why? Because lions are the top of the food chain, if you don't count people. Ranging from 250 to 500 pounds, these massive cats aren't the fastest creatures, but they are rather sneaky. Lionesses (female lions) do most of the hunting. They work in groups to surround a herd quietly, trying hard to remain hidden. Then, when a weak or slow member of the herd breaks away from the group, the lionesses pounce and almost instantly kill their victim.

God says Satan is like a roaring lion who wants to destroy you. Just as the lioness hunts her prey, Satan wants to separate you from the group—God's family—so he can trick you with his lies. If you start listening to him, he can crush your faith. So not only do you need to be brave, you also need to stay strong. That's why it's so important to stay connected to God and His people at all times. God—your ultimate source of strength—and His people will help you stand strong against the enemy. Because he is always on the hunt!

A BRAVE GIRL'S PRAYER

Lord, help me stay connected to You, fill me with Your
strength, and protect me from Satan's schemes.

WHO'S THE BRAVEST OF THEM ALL?

Be strong in the Lord and in his great power.

EPHESIANS 6:10

The bravest person I know is _____

_____

The thing that makes this person so brave is _____

_____

_____

I know that God helps by _____

_____

_____

Attach or draw a picture of that person here.

NOW WHaT?

If we confess our sins, He will forgive our sins. . . . He will make us clean from all the wrongs we have done.

1 JOHN 1:9

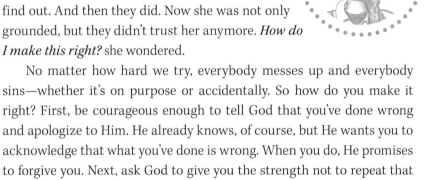

Abbie had completely blown it—and she knew it. Her parents had said she couldn't get a certain new app for her phone, but she'd secretly downloaded it anyway, hoping they wouldn't find out. And then they did. Now she was not only grounded, but they didn't trust her anymore. *How do I make this right?* she wondered.

No matter how hard we try, everybody messes up and everybody sins—whether it's on purpose or accidentally. So how do you make it right? First, be courageous enough to tell God that you've done wrong and apologize to Him. He already knows, of course, but He wants you to acknowledge that what you've done is wrong. When you do, He promises to forgive you. Next, ask God to give you the strength not to repeat that sin. Finally, be brave and try to make things right with the people in your life. Admit your sins and apologize to them too. It might take a little time to regain their trust, but you're off to a great start!

A BRaVE GIRL'S PRaYER

God, when I mess up, help me come straight to You to make things right again.

CRABBY HABITS

Wear God's armor so that you can fight
against the devil's evil tricks.

EPHESIANS 6:11

Have you ever waded in the surf, searching for seashells, only to find one with a crab-like creature inside? If so, you've discovered a hermit crab. But did you know that hermit crabs don't grow their own shells? They borrow shells from sea snails. When hermit crabs outgrow their shells, they *molt*, meaning they switch to larger shells. Until he finds a new shell, the soft hermit crab is vulnerable to predators.

Like hermit crabs, we're vulnerable to our enemy, Satan. But God has given us a "shell" to protect us too: the armor of God. (Read about it in Ephesians 6, where Paul described the belt of truth, breastplate of righteousness, sword of the Spirit, helmet of salvation, shield of faith, and shoes of peace.) As long as we're in the habit of covering ourselves with our armor and fighting the lies of the enemy with the truth of God's Word, we can be brave—knowing we are protected and free to grow and encourage others to put on their special armor too.

A BRAVE GIRL'S PRAYER

Jesus, thank You for giving me the armor of
God to help protect me from harm.

SUPERHERO YOU

Be strong in the Lord and in His great power.

EPHESIANS 6:10

The Bible says you are in a war—not against people, but against the devil and the darkness of evil (Ephesians 6:12). Imagine you're a superhero for God, charging off to fight that battle.

What would your armor be? _____

_____

_____

What would your superpowers be and **Who** (hint, hint) would you get them from? _____

_____

_____

_____

_____

What would your superhero you look like? _____

_____

_____

_____

_____

A BIGGER PLAN

"I have good plans for you. I don't plan to hurt
you. I plan to give you hope and a good future."

JEREMIAH 29:11

Wow! Amy thought. *Today did not turn out the way I wanted. I worked so hard on that science project. I just knew I'd win and get to go to the state competition. But everything went wrong. I am so frustrated and disappointed! This whole thing is completely hopeless!*

Amy had a really bad day. It happens to everyone. We work hard and try to do what's right, then it blows up in our faces. But it's okay—or, at least, it will be. That's because God's got a bigger plan.

When things don't work out the way you think they should, be grateful. Yes, *grateful*! Because that means God has something even better planned for you. You might see it right away, or it may take a little while. Until then, be brave, stand strong, and trust God. He'll only do what's best for you.

A BRAVE GIRL'S PRAYER

God, I know You've got good things planned for
my life. Please give me the courage to trust
that Your plans are the best plans of all.

THE PERFECT HIDING SPOT

I will come to you as a bird comes for
protection under its mother's wings
until the trouble has passed.

PSALM 57:1

Do you ever feel like playing hide-and-seek (minus the seek part) with the whole world? Maybe it's been a really bad day, or you know someone is upset with you. Or maybe it's been a great day, but now you're just plain tired and you want to hide away for a little while. It happens to us all, and God understands. He's even got the perfect hiding spot for you.

Where is that hiding spot? It's under His wings. Imagine a baby bird, all snuggled up under its mother's wings. She's safe and warm and loved. Nothing can trouble or harm her there. Now imagine that baby bird is you. When you turn to God for help and for rest, He pulls you in close and snuggles you under His wings. You're safe and warm and loved.

Yes, there are so many times in life when you will need to be brave, but remember, it's also okay to take time to hide and to rest under God's wings.

A BRAVE GIRL'S PRAYER

Thank You, Lord, for giving me a place to hide
away from the world for a while. I know I am
safe and loved when I'm under Your wings.

HELPING HUGS

There is a time to hug. . . . There is a
time to be silent and a time to speak.

ECCLESIASTES 3:5, 7

Emily watched her mom put down the telephone and sit down on the couch. Her eyes were filled with tears.

"Mom, are you okay?" Emily asked.

"Oh, honey, I just found out a friend of mine is very sick," her mom said, wiping her eyes.

Emily didn't know what to say, so she just sat down next to her mom and wrapped her in a big hug. In her heart, she prayed for her mom and her friend.

Have you ever found yourself in a situation when you didn't know what to say? Maybe your mom had an upsetting phone call, like Emily's mom did. Or your dad had trouble at work, or a friend just had a really rotten day. You know you can't fix the problem, and saying "I'm sorry" doesn't seem like enough. Then it might be time for a hug. When the people you love are hurting, a hug helps them know they're not alone, and that you care about them. It can give them the strength they need to be brave. So the next time words fail you, try a hug instead.

A BRAVE GIRL'S PRAYER

Lord, when I'm hurting You give me comfort.
Help me comfort others too.

HUGS FOR ALL!

We love because God first loved us.

1 JOHN 4:19

To me, a hug means _____

_____

_____

_____

When I hug someone, what I'm really saying is _____

_____

_____

_____

The person who gives the very best hugs _____

_____

When I'm sad, this is who I find for a hug _____

_____

The best hug I ever got _____

_____

If I could have a hug from anyone, it would be _____

_____

_____

SCENTS OF GREATNESS

The teaching about the cross seems foolish
to those who are lost. But to us who are
being saved it is the power of God.

1 CORINTHIANS 1:18

Lemurs are ring-tailed primates from Madagascar known for their good looks, lively antics, and leaping abilities. But what lemur lovers may not know is how they smell. Male lemurs use scent glands to coat their tails with a pungent and powerful secretion to make them more attractive to females. Though to us the scent is terrible, the female lemur thinks it's terrific! The male with the strongest scent usually wins the girl.

God says our lives can have a similar effect when it comes to telling people about Jesus. For those people still fighting God, who don't want to follow Him, they think the message of the gospel stinks! But for those people who are ready to hear about Jesus, it's a sweet scent. And Jesus says that sharing His message with others is like a beautiful perfume to Him too. Don't worry about how people may react to God's message—be brave and fill the world with the fragrance of Christ!

A BRAVE GIRL'S PRAYER

God, help me to be brave enough to share Your
beautiful message of hope with everyone I meet.

THE NAMES OF THE BRAVE

"I have called you by name, and you are mine."

ISAIAH 43:1

God thinks you're so special, He uses all kinds of names to let you know who you are to Him. His love for you is steady and true—and it can give you the courage to be steady and true too!

Unscramble the words below and understand just how deeply God cares for you—let that knowledge make you brave!

SCHONE _____ 1 Peter 2:9

AYPHP _____ Psalm 32:1

YHLO _____ Isaiah 62:12

NODLERWFU _____ Psalm 139:14

IEMN _____ Isaiah 43:1

IHS HICLREND _____ Ephesians 1:5

INFRGVEO _____ Romans 4:7

EMAD EWN _____ 2 Corinthians 5:17

EBALUIFUT _____ Song of Solomon 4:7

RSECIPOU _____ Isaiah 43:4

HODNORE _____ Isaiah 43:4

Answers: chosen, happy, holy, wonderful, Mine, His children, forgiven, made new, beautiful, precious, honored

•173•

Team up on the Devil

The Lord watches over those who follow Him. He
frees them from the power of the wicked.

PSALM 97:10

There's something about the story of Esther that you may not have noticed: the rivalry between Haman (the bad guy who wanted to kill the Jews) and Mordecai (the God-fearing Jew who raised Esther). Haman wanted everyone to think he was important. He even made people bow to him. Mordecai wouldn't obey, because he only bowed to God. So Haman plotted to kill not just Mordecai but *all* the Jews. That's when a new team formed to turn things around. Mordecai and Esther joined together with all the Jews to fast and pray secretly. Then Esther planned a way to alert the king and upset Haman's plans. God was on His people's side, and Haman was defeated when Esther exposed his evil plan.

Esther showed incredible bravery, but her story is also about Mordecai and the other Jews who came together, prayed, and—with God's power—stopped Haman's plan. In other words, it was a total team effort. And that's the same way God wants His people to fight Satan's schemes today.

When you're faced with trouble and need to be brave, don't set off on your own. Team up on the devil, and go to God first!

A Brave Girl's Prayer

God, I want to be part of Your team. Show me how
I can work with others to do Your will today.

WHO'S YOUR TEAM?

Give yourselves to God. Stand against the
devil, and the devil will run away from you.

JAMES 4:7

Make a list of people you'd like to be on your team, and list their
strengths.

Name: _____

Strength: _____

Name: _____

Strength: _____

Name: _____

Strength: _____

Name: _____

Strength: _____

Why did you choose these specific people to be on your team? _____

_____

_____

What positive influences can you bring to your team? _____

_____

_____

_____

MOONLIGHT MADNESS

He gave us light by letting us know the glory
of God that is in the face of Christ.

2 CORINTHIANS 4:6

If you're watching at just the right time of night, in just the right place along the beach, you can witness a marching miracle. Hundreds of newly hatched baby sea turtles poke through the sand and start their quest for the ocean.

Baby sea turtles have a problem, though. Instinct tells them to head toward the light, which is a wonderful GPS feature when the moon is full and bright. But sometimes they hatch near streetlights that give off a bright glow and look a lot like the moon to a baby turtle. Confused, the turtles tragically flip and flop onto busy streets instead of into the sea!

In some ways, we're like those turtles. We're drawn to the fake beauty of sinful things—just as those baby turtles are drawn to the fake "moon" of streetlights. We can get confused and dazzled by the very things that can hurt us the most. God tells us to fix our eyes on Him and His perfect light.

It won't always be easy, and you'll have to stay strong. But God will always be there to help you and lead you to where you need to be.

A BRAVE GIRL'S PRAYER

God, Your Word is a light for my path.
Thank You for leading me to life!

Carried Away

The Lord takes care of His people like a
shepherd. He gathers the people like lambs
in His arms. He carries them close to Him.

ISAIAH 40:11

Have you ever had your mom or dad carry you? Maybe when you were younger, you were carried up to bed. Or perhaps you were feeling lost and small in a crowd, and your dad lifted you on his shoulders to see. Or maybe you were hurt, and your mom held you until you felt better. It's a wonderful feeling, isn't it? It's so much easier to be brave when you're safe in the arms of someone you trust.

That's what God does for us too. When we're tired, He scoops us up and carries us so that we can rest. When we're feeling small and not very important, He lifts us up and reminds us that we're always important to Him. And when we're hurt, He gathers us in His arms and carries us close to His heart until the hurt goes away. We can be brave because God's got us safely in His arms.

Just as a loving parent takes care of a child, God takes care of His child—and that's you!

A Brave Girl's Prayer

Lord, when I'm feeling tired or lonely or hurt, please help
me remember You're here with me to carry me through.

JOINT EFFORT

At the sound of the trumpets and the people's shout, the walls fell.

JOSHUA 6:20

Last night our youth group leader asked us if we'd ever thought about why God's plan to defeat Jericho was so *strange* (Joshua 6). Here's how it went:

LEADER: So what did God ask them to do?

HONOR: God told them to march around the city one time each day for six days, and on the seventh day, march around it seven times. Then they were supposed to blow trumpets, shout, and rush in to capture the city when the walls fell.

GRACIE: I bet those people from Jericho thought they were nuts.

HOPE: Yeah, until the walls came crashing down! But why did they have to keep walking around the city?

GLORY: And be silent the whole time until the time they could shout? If I'd been there, my big mouth would've ruined the whole thing.

FAITH: That's just it! They had to work together to follow God's plan. God wanted them to learn to work together and trust Him.

It takes courage to trust God and His ways—especially when they don't make sense to you. The next time you don't understand God's plans, remember those flattened walls of Jericho. Then be strong, and follow Him!

A BRAVE GIRL'S PRAYER

God, please give me the courage to stick with
Your people and trust Your plans.

A SWEET CONNECTION

THe smoke FRom tHe iNceNse weNt up FRom
tHe aNgel's HaNd to God. It weNt up
witH tHe pRayeRs of God's people.

REVELATION 8:4

To God, the sweetest smells in all the world are the prayers of His people! The Old Testament talks about people burning incense—a mixture of fragrant herbs—when they worshipped God. And Revelation says our prayers rise up before God's throne, just like incense in the temple. Prayer is a beautiful offering from us to God.

Prayer also connects us to God and helps us realize how much we need Him. It helps us to be filled with His power, His purpose, and His peace. Use the ideas below to help you come closer to God and learn to pray about what matters most to Him.

- THe book of Psalms is a collection of pRayeRs and soNgs. EacH day, cHoose a diffeReNt psalm to Read.

- CHoose a psalm to RewRite iN youR owN woRds, offeRiNg it as youR pRayeR to God.

- PRay foR wisdom to kNow How and wHat to pRay. Ask tHe Holy SpiRit to lead youR tHougHts and woRds.

A BRave GiRl's PRayeR

LoRd, tHaNk You foR listeNiNg to me!

MY PRAYER CONNECTIONS

Pray for all people. Ask God for the things
people need, and be thankful to Him.

1 TIMOTHY 2:1

Think of all the people and things you would like to pray for, and write them in the appropriate box. Then watch to see how God answers your prayers.

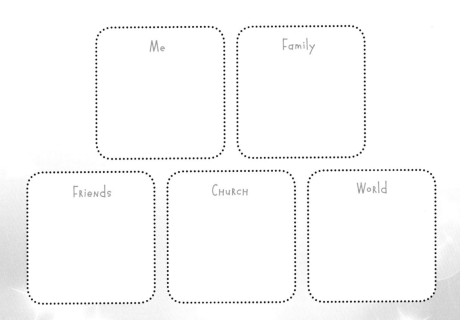

HEAVENLY WISDOM

I always pRay to tHe God of ouR LoRd Jesus
CHRist . . . tHat He will give you a spiRit tHat
will make you wise in tHe knowledge of God.

Jane could make straight *As* without even studying. But at home, Jane wasn't feeling so smart. Her parents fought a lot, but she didn't know what to do. Should she talk to them, or would it be better to stay quiet? Could she trust her friend with this information, or would her friend gossip behind her back? Nothing in her schoolbooks could help Jane solve this real-life problem.

WHat would you say Jane needs to do in tHis situation? _____

_____

_____

WHy do you tHink tHat? _____

_____

_____

How can Jane ever know the right thing to do? On her own, she can't. Jane needs wisdom, but she doesn't have it. Wisdom is far different from being smart. Wisdom is understanding life from God's perspective and knowing and following His directions.

Where do we get wisdom? From God! If we simply ask Him for wisdom, He promises to give it to us. Sometimes He uses the Bible to give us the wisdom. Sometimes He guides us through trusted parents or leaders who know His ways. Sometimes He simply works out the situation so we see His power. But God is always faithful to give us His heavenly wisdom to work through our earthly troubles.

A BRAVE GIRL'S PRAYER

Lord, help me be humble and turn to You for wisdom, so I can know what I should do.

WHAT TO DO?

The Lord says, "I will make you wise. I will show you where to go. I will guide you and watch over you."

PSALM 32:8

Being brave is no good if you don't know the right thing to do! Fortunately, God is always there to lead the way. Look up these verses on wisdom. What do they say? Use them to write your own prayer for wisdom below.

James 1:5 _____

_____

_____

2 Chronicles 1:11-12 _____

_____

_____

Job 12:13 _____

_____

_____

Psalm 37:30 _____

_____

_____

Psalm 104:24 _____

_____

_____

Psalm 111:10 _____

_____

_____

1 Corinthians 3:19 _____

_____

_____

James 3:17 _____

_____

_____

MY PRAYER

"You must love each other as I have loved you."

JOHN 13:34

If someone asked you to describe a Christian, what would you say? You'd probably mention things like "reads the Bible," "prays," "goes to church," or even "does good things for people." Those are all signs that people might have given their lives to Jesus. But when you think about it, lots of people who don't claim to be Christians live good lives. And many other religions teach that you have to do good works and stay away from bad behaviors.

Jesus says His children will be known by our love—love for Jesus, love for other believers, and love for those who don't know Him. The ability to love like that takes great courage—the kind of courage that can only come from the Holy Spirit of God, who lives inside us.

Ask God to help you consider your words and your actions, and make sure they show His love. God will pour out His love through you as you bravely reach out to others who need to know Him! And everyone will know you're His child by the courageous, shining light of your love.

A BRAVE GIRL'S PRAYER

Jesus, fill me with Your love for others, and help
me to be brave enough to let it shine.

BE BOLDLY BEAUTIFUL

Our physical body is becoming older and weaker,
but our spirit inside us is made new every day.

2 CORINTHIANS 4:16

Have you ever been in the makeup aisle at the store? There's every kind of powder, cream, and lotion imaginable, and they all promise to make you beautiful. But real beauty doesn't come in a jar or a tube. Real beauty comes from being brave enough to be the girl God wants you to be—and it happens from the inside out.

God is slowly changing us from the ugliness of our sin to the beautiful goodness of His Son. The more we trust and obey God, the more we realize how much we need Jesus and the more beautiful we become. We actually begin to think, talk, and act more like Jesus and less like our old, selfish selves. And we become beautiful mirrors of God's never-ending affection for His people.

True beauty can't be bought in the makeup aisle. It only comes from boldly loving Jesus and courageously living for Him. That kind of beauty not only makes us shine, but it also lasts for all eternity in heaven with Jesus.

A BRAVE GIRL'S PRAYER

Lord, change me from the inside out, and make
me Your kind of beautiful forever.

YEAH . . . I'M AWESOME!

The Lord does great things.

PSALM 111:2

I am so awesome at _____

_____

My friends say I'm awesome at _____

_____

My family says I'm awesome at _____

_____

I really wish I were awesome at _____

_____

I'm not-so-awesome at _____

_____

I love that I can _____

_____

God thinks I'm awesome because _____

_____

_____

_____

TO SEE OR NOT TO SEE

FaitH means being suRe of tHe tHings we
HOPE foR. And faitH means knowing tHat
sometHing is Real even if we do Not see it.

HEBREWS 11:1

Do you believe in things you can't see? Of course you do! In fact, we all do. We believe in things like gravity and air and wind. We can't see them, but we see what they do and how they make things move. We also believe in things like Mars and atoms and deep-water anemone. We probably can't see them for ourselves, but others have. They tell us about them and may even have pictures.

Faith in God is also believing in what we cannot see. We cannot see God's face, but we can see Him in the wonders of this world He's made. We can't hear His voice, but others did. And they wrote down God's words for us to read. We can't touch His hand, but we can feel where His hand touches our lives with love and joy, with His comfort and His peace. Believe, Brave Girl . . . and one day, you will see the One you have believed.

A BRAVE GIRL'S PRAYER

God, I caNNot see You, but I know You aRe Real. Give me tHe
couRage to Recognize and to believe tHe pRoof all aRound me.

A HOME FOR THE BRAVE

"There are many rooms in my Father's house.
I would not tell you this if it were not true.
I am going there to prepare a place for you."

JOHN 14:2

Picture in your mind a big, beautiful house. Everything looks lovely, but when you look closer, you realize the walls are cracked and they aren't securely connected to the floor—or to each other! How long could a wobbly house like that stand? You don't have to be a construction expert to know that's not good!

Jesus tells us that He is the foundation we should build our lives on. He won't ever crack or wobble like the things of this world—and when you depend on Him to make you strong, you won't either.

The fact is you were created to be a part of His kingdom. Without you, there's a hole where your presence should be. *You* are a much-needed and even-more-wanted part of the kingdom of God. Claim His promises for your own. It will take some courage, a lot of determination and perseverance—and yes, you'll definitely have to be brave. But when you build your life on the foundation of Jesus, He'll build a room in heaven for you.

A BRAVE GIRL'S PRAYER

Jesus, teach me to build my life on You so that
one day I can live with You always.

DEAR ME . . .

You've learned so much about being brave and what it really means. Now write a letter to your past self, praising yourself for the times you were brave and forgiving yourself for the times you were not-so-brave.

DEAR FUTURE ME . . .

Write a letter to your future self, reminding yourself to be brave.

The Lord your God is with you.
The mighty One will save you.
The Lord will be happy with you.
You will rest in His love.
He will sing and be joyful about you.

ZEPHANIAH 3:17

Brave Girls is a brand from Tommy Nelson

that strives to pour the love and truth of God's Word into the lives of young girls, equipping them with the knowledge they need to grow into young women who are confident in Christ.

BRAVE GIRLS BIBLE STORIES

Learn the Bible alongside the Brave Girls, who are just like you! Each devotion begins with an introduction from a Brave Girl, dives into a story about a brave (or not-so-brave) woman of the Bible, and closes with some insight from the Brave Girl character.

BRAVE GIRLS BIBLE

This beautifully illustrated, two-color, expanded-content ICB study Bible features characters from the Brave Girls brand who are eager to teach readers about the Word of God and how they can apply the Bible to their everyday lives.

Ready for More Brave Girls Devotions and Stories?

BRAVE GIRLS 365 DEVOTIONAL

Join the Brave Girls as they discover that the closer they are to God, the more He makes ordinary girls like them strong and courageous!

Brave Girls Devotionals:
BETTER THAN PERFECT, FAITHFUL FRIENDS, AND BEAUTIFUL YOU

The Brave Girls are back! These three 90-day devotionals let readers learn more about the lives of the Brave Girls and how they tackle important issues like being a good friend and knowing God loves you no matter what.

BRAVE GIRLS CONFIDENTIAL

Are you ready to bring out the Brave Girl in you? Join the Brave Girls as they tell stories and share secrets—and learn all about faith and friendship.